PARACHUTE MOVEMENT ACTIVITIES

A COMPLETE PARACHUTE MOVEMENT PROGRAM
FOR ELEMENTARY GRADES AND BEYOND

by

RON FRENCH and MICHAEL HORVAT

EDITOR
Frank Alexander

ARTIST
Dawn Bates

Published by FRONT ROW EXPERIENCE, 540 Discovery Bay Blvd., Byron, Calif. 94514

2,000 BOOKS IN PRINT AS OF 1990

Copyright © 1983 RON FRENCH & MICHAEL HORVAT

ISBN 0-915256-13-4

Published

by

FRONT ROW EXPERIENCE
540 Discovery Bay Blvd.
Byron, California 94514

ACKNOWLEDGEMENTS

We would like to acknowledge those individuals whose assistance enhanced the quality of the manuscript. First Dr. Sandy Beveridge, Mr. Freddie Bennett, Dr. Hester Henderson, Ms. Terri Horvat, Mr. Brent Mangus, and Dr. Barbara West who, based on their teaching experiences with children and youth, critically reviewed the manuscript. Second Ms. Kelly French for her patience in demonstrating the numerous motor patterns and providing several parachute activity ideas. Lastly, we are indebted to Mrs. Dawn Bates for her illustrations which clearly depict the parachute activities.

ABOUT THE AUTHORS

Dr. Michael A. Horvat was awarded his bachelor and master's degrees from the University of North Carolina majoring in physical education and minoring in health. He received his doctorate from the University of Utah majoring in physical education and minoring in special education.

Presently Dr. Horvat is an associate professor in the departments of Physical Education and Special Education at the University of Nevada, Las Vegas, where he is the coordinator of the Special Physical Education undergraduate and graduate programs. His teaching responsibilities are in both the areas of physical education for special populations and motor development. In the summers he is the director of a sports and recreation program at the University for children and youth.

Dr. Ron French received his bachelor and master of science degrees in physical education while minoring in biology from the Humboldt State College. He received his doctorate from the University of California at Los Angeles in special education, minoring in physical education and educational administration.

Presently Dr. French is an associate professor in the Department of Physical Education at the University of Utah where he is responsible for the Special Physical Education Training Program and the Director of Graduate Studies. Previously he was a motor performance specialist for the Manhattan School District in California and an assistant professor in physical education at Brockport College in New York where he taught courses in special physical education and elementary physical education.

CONTENTS

INTRODUCTION

The invention of the parachute has been credited to Leonardo da Vinci in the late 15th century. At this time it was just an idea in pictorial form for maintaining an individual aloft for a short period of time.

The principle behind the invention was that the umbrella shape of the canopy would allow air to be trapped causing a resistance to the gravitational pull. This in turn reduced the rate of speed of the falling object. In 1783, Montgolfier dropped an animal by parachute from a tower, then Louis Lenormard parachuted from the same tower. Both were successful. This proved that animals and humans could descend from great heights unharmed.

With the invention of the balloon in the 18th and aircraft in the early 20th century, the idea of a parachute was transformed into a practical piece of equipment. It is now used for emergency jumps, to deliver cargo (food/medicine), for special military use, as brakes for some planes and racing cars, and for sports (sky diving) competition.

Within the last 2 decades, the parachute has also become a integral component of creative physical education and recreation programs for individuals ranging from preschool children to senior citizens (Hanson, 1980, Schurr, 1980), including those with handicapping conditions.

Many educators and recreators who are in charge of physical education type programs continually utilize the same activities day after day to meet their specific program objectives even though the participant's motivational level may gradually decrease. Often, the versatility of the parachute has been overlooked by the same educators and recreators. It can be, however, an exciting alternative in reaching the program objectives. For instance, if the participants become bored with performing sit-ups or running a lap, parachute activities can be used intermittently to motivate the participants and still develop abdominal strength and cardiorespiratory endurance.

1

BENEFITS OF PARACHUTE ACTIVITIES

There are numerous benefits to incorporating the parachute into a physical education or recreation program. These benefits can be categorized into 4 developmental
areas: 1) physical, 2) motor, 3) social-emotional, and 4) academic.

PHYSICAL DEVELOPMENT BENEFITS

Physical activity is necessary for maximum physical development. Through a
structured exercise program, muscle tissue and bone growth are stimulated.
The physique of the individual, particularly those who are overweight, may also
be influenced by physical activity. Through a well-planned program muscular
strength, muscular endurance, flexibility, and cardiorespiratory endurance can
be developed and maintained allowing each individual to function at their op-
timal level of fitness for daily living.

Most physical fitness activities such as aerobic dancing and jogging promote
cardiorespiratory endurance; pull-ups and sit-ups can develop muscular strength
and endurance; bending, twisting, and stretching activities can develop flexibility. All these activities can be incorporated into a parachute activity
program.

MOTOR DEVELOPMENT BENEFITS

Competent professionals can assist each individual develop, rehabilitate, or
maintain the most efficient motor patterns by incorporating developmentally
appropriate motor skills into parachute activities such as jumping, running,
and skipping. Additionally, concepts which increase perceptual awareness such
as left, right, high, low, stop, go, up and down, over and under can easily
be incorporated into creative parachute activities to enhance motor development.
Rhythms and dances with circle formations can also be taught using the parachute.

Motor skills which are deficient because of injury or neglect can be rehabili-
tated or maintained by utilizing the parachute activities. It must be remembered, however, that the parachute activities are a medium for restoring function following an injury and they should be continued in order to maintain the
gains from the increased level of activity.

SOCIAL-EMOTIONAL DEVELOPMENT BENEFITS

Physical education and recreation personnel can also assist individuals learn
desirable ways to deal with others and provide opportunities for social interaction. Most physical activities are emotionally charged. For instance, within a brief time during a physical activity an individual's attitude can change
from extreme disappointment to elation and back again. Individuals can learn
to manage these and other behaviors appropriately through the guidance of the
physical educator and recreator. They can also learn rules inherent in each
activity.

Parachute activities can become one of the primary vehicles in developing social and emotional skills by increasing the social interaction among participants. In addition, many physical activities for young children require the
use of scatter formations. For many children, the lack of structure inherent
in this type of formation can create many non-participants who stand or sit on

the perimeter or in the middle of an activity observing or attending to irrelevant stimuli while the other children actively participate. While engaging in a parachute activity, each child is assigned a section of the parachute which he/she must grasp. When the educator or recreator says, "walk clockwise while grasping the parachute with your left hand," each child generally will participate or the object they are holding will move with or without them.

Numerous parachute activities are excellent for preschool aged children functioning at a parallel social level. The social sequence level of development can be enhanced through cooperative efforts of children by sharing holding duties, changing positions, performing activity in unison, or tug-of-war. In other activities each child must stand side by side but they do not directly interact with one another. For older individuals, the parachute can be an excellent ice breaker and up-beat activity which can stimulate movement and enhance the development of social interactions. It also can serve to vent frustrations.

ACADEMIC DEVELOPMENT BENEFITS
Parachute activities can enhance academic development. Each time an individual participates in a game or sport, thinking is required. Some authorities contend that the level of physical fitness is related to intellectual accomplishments, particularly mental alertness and concentration.

Aside from the use of developing perceptual concepts as indicated earlier, one of the most interesting uses of the parachute for children and youth is the utilization of academic concepts. For example, mathematics can easily be incorporated into parachutes by assigning each player a number. The group leader then calls out a problem such as $9 - 4 = ?$ The player assigned the number which is the correct answer then has to perform a task under the parachute. Steal-The-Bacon, Capture-The-Flag, or other game activities can also be utilized to implement academic concepts. In addition to learning new concepts, parachute activities can be used to reinforce concepts taught in the classroom or practice already mastered skills.

TEACHING SUGGESTIONS

1) Make sure you establish complete control of the participants before any parachute activity begins. It is recommended that before the activity begins the group leader should spread and stretch out the parachute. When the activity is initiated the participants are to go to the parachute, stand or kneel around it, and grasp the outer ridge with both hands. Do not let any participant run under or over it or put their hands or head through the center hole. It is important to re-establish complete control before starting a new activity.

2) Spread the parachute on the floor. Seat each participant evenly around the parachute (approximately 2 to 3 feet apart) during the instructional portion of the activity.

3) Begin each activity with the command, "Ready, Go!". "Ready" allows the participants an opportunity to prepare for the activity and "Go" enables everyone to commence the activity at the same time (Evans, 1979).

4) Repeat each activity several times.

5) Continually have them alternate the hand grips to develop different muscle groups: a) palms up, b) palms down, c) one palm up, one palm down, and d) cross over.

6) Avoid confusion by structuring an easy transition into and out of your activities.

7) Emphasize holding onto the parachute during the entire length of the activity. This will allow a more coordinated effort between the participants.

8) Utilize activities which are motivating for the participants. For example, young children enjoy activities which are active and involve imagination. Older participants, on the other hand, may enjoy activities which predominately involve social interaction such as dances.

9) Challenge the participants to add and improvise parachute activities creating new games and activities.

10) Continually remind participants where they are going (left to right, etc.).

11) Usually 40 to 50 individuals can perform parachute activities at one time using a large parachute (24 ft diameter plus). However, approximately 20 elementary-aged children or 10 to 12 teenagers or adults can effectively manage the parachute to perform most activities. Smaller parachutes are available (see Resources section of the book) for groups of 6 to 8 participants. It should be noted that the action of the parachute is reduced when a smaller parachute is used. If it seems that there are not enough participants to perform activities and a smaller chute is not available, you can roll up the edges of the parachute to make it smaller. This will allow for better control and manageability of the parachute.

12) Make sure the participants are familiar with the parachute and understand the terminology you use for each activity.

13) Teach only the activities which are simple and clearly understood, then expand into the more complex actions. In many cases demonstrations may be needed.

14) Initially you should teach each activity without the use of records. Once most of the participants understand the instructions and movement patterns then incorporate records. The voice on the record becomes a teacher aide and frees the group leader to assist those participants who may have problems.

15) When balls are used, retrieve them by selecting 2 or 3 ball retrievers.

16) Vary the activities according to the physical fitness level of the participants and change tempos or activities to motivate the participants. Do not allow the participants to become over fatigued.

17) Make sure the participants take their shoes off when the activity requires them to walk on the parachute. And even go farther by taking socks off since it could be slippery with stocking feet. In general, you may want to have participants perform *all* activities in their bare feet in order to add another dimension of tactile stimulation.

18) Never allow participants to strike the parachute.

19) Clean the parachute regularly since dirt can deteriorate the material.

20) Repair any tear by sewing or ironing on nylon patches immediately after it is torn.

ACTIVITIES FOR SPECIAL POPULATIONS

If you are using parachute activities with individuals with special needs, you should be aware of some basic programmatic considerations in designing parachute activities. Presented below are a variety of considerations listed by the specific handicapping condition.*

CONDITIONS	PARTICIPATION CONSIDERATIONS FOR PARACHUTE ACTIVITIES*
ASTHMA	1) Obtain physician's written consent. 2) Attacks (wheezing, coughing, etc.) can be brought about by strenuous physical activities and/or emotional stressful (excitement; highly competitive) parachute activities. 3) Depending on the cause of the attack, activity area may have to be free from dust or simply not be a grassy area. 4) Understand the effects of medication on the performance of parachute activities, some interfere with the ability to balance (refer to Table 1 on page 7).
HARD OF HEARING AND DEAF	1) Demonstrate and/or physically move participants through activities. 2) Use a buddy system. 3) Provide warning signals.
CARDIAC DISORDER	1) Obtain physician's written consent. 2) Assess physical fitness level before entering the program. 3) Take pulse before and after each parachute activity, if necessary. 4) Teach each participant how to take her or his own pulse. 5) Provide short rest periods.

----

* Modified from: Bishop, P. and French, R. Physical Education For Handicapped Children: Considerations For Participation. In Bishop, P. and Fois, P. (Eds.). Adapted Physical Education. Resource Manual. Kearney, NE: Kearney State College, Special Education Dept., 1981, 16-22.

6) Avoid parachute activities which involve endurance (such as performing ripples and waves for 10 minutes) unless you have medical consent.

7) Isometric (applying constant pressure against or away from an inmovable object) parachute activities such as pulling the edge of the parachute should not be tried.

CEREBRAL PALSY

1) Obtain physician's written consent and/or assistance of a physical or occupational therapist.

2) Parachute activities which may overstimulate (that is, too much activity or excitement) or overfatigue participants are sometimes not recommended for cerebral palsied participants.

3) Avoid parachute activities which place the participant in a position which could bring about an abnormal reflex. For instance, a child may have problems crawling. The problem may not be one of low fitness or balance but caused by an abnormal reflex (symmetrical tonic neck reflex) that should have disappeared during infancy. This reflex involves the arms flexing (bending) and the legs extending when the head is in the down position. The activity should be eliminated or you must constantly remind the child to keep his or her head up and look forward.

4) Be careful about the grasp on the parachute. Some cerebral palsied individuals may not have the ability to properly release the parachute. This could cause damage to the muscles, tendons, and/or ligaments in the hands.

CYSTIC FIBROSIS

1) Obtain physician's written consent.

2) Certain parachute activities which strengthen shoulder muscles are encouraged.

3) Endurance parachute activities should be prescribed on an individual basis since some individual's ability to endure some activities could be very low.

DEPRESSION

1) Understand the effect of medication. Many medications that are frequently prescribed may be hazardous in performing some parachute activities (refer to Table 1 on page 7).

2. Encourage activity.

DIABETES

1) Obtain physician's written consent.

2) Balance the amount of physical activity with insulin (believed to allow nutrients into cells) use.

3) Understand the effects of medication, such as fatigue and unsteady gait on performing specific activities (refer to Table 1 on page 8).

HYPERACTIVITY

1) See "Depression" considerations previously presented and Table 1 on page .

2) Supervise closely.

MULTIPLE SCLEROSIS

1) Obtain physician's written consent.

2) Ability to perform parachute activities changes with periods of remission. The group leaders must constantly reevaluate the activities which are selected for a person with this condition.

CONDITIONS	PARTICIPATION CONSIDERATIONS FOR PARACHUTE ACTIVITIES (continued)

MUSCULAR DYSTROPHY

1) With physician's written consent.
2) Avoid performing parachute activities in environments (that is, cold, damp places, etc.) where there is a probability of developing respiratory infection.
3) Endurance parachute activities are recommended to maintain the highest level of fitness.

PREGNANCY

1) There are few restrictions, but caution must be taken in parachute activities that require a high degree of agility (quick changes in direction), since the center of gravity is constantly changing throughout the pregnancy.
2) Activities which place additional strain on the low back should be avoided.

SEIZURES (Epilepsy)

1) Obtain physician's written consent.
2) You should be aware of first aid procedures: a) Remain calm; b) If possible, lower participant to the ground; c) Place in cushioned area, if possible; d) Clear obstacles to prevent bodily injury; e) Tilt the head to one side, but never force it; f) Loosen any tight clothing; g) Observe seizure to provide information to medical personnel; h) Allow the person time to rest after the seizure (French & Jansma, 1982).

PARTIALLY SIGHTED AND BLIND

1) Familiarize the participant with the environment. For instance, let the student feel the chute and walk around the instructional area.
2) Participants with glaucoma (excessive pressure in the eye ball) should not perform parachute activities that require performing isometric (applying constant pressure against or away from an immovable object) exercises such as lifting another participant with full exertion.
3) Participants with a detached retina (receives light rays and converts images into nerve impulses to send to the brain) should not perform parachute activities that require a sudden turning of the head or any activities which may cause a blow to the head such as dodge ball.
4) Use verbal cues (that is, bell or whistle) to stop and start the activity.
5) Use the buddy system.

TABLE 1 - EFFECTS OF SPECIFIC MEDICATION ON PHYSICAL AND MOTOR PERFORMANCE

Purpose	Medication (Trade Name)	Possible Side Effects
Asthma	Actifed, Dimetapp, Drixol, and Ornade	Nervousness, dizziness, uncoordination, confusion, and blurred vision
Cardiac Condition	Ser-Ap-Es	Drowsiness, blurred vision, muscle aches, and muscle tremors
Depression	Elavil and Tofranil	Blurred vision, confusion, disorientation, and drowsiness

TABLE 1 (continued)

Purpose	Medication (Trade Name)	Possible Side Effects
Diabetes	Diabenese and Orinase	Weakness, fatigue, dizziness, and unsteady gait
Hyperactivity	Ritalin	Dizziness, blurred vision, confusion, and drowsiness
	Dexedrine	Blurred vision, confusion, disorientation, drowsiness, and weight loss
Seizures (Epilepsy)	Lummal	Dizziness and drowsiness
	Dilantin	Mental confusion, dizziness, fatigue, and visual disturbances

BASIC PARACHUTE TERMINOLOGY

There are several fundamental terms and activities which are used with the parachute that the group leader must know before initiating a structured program. When appropriate, the following basic terminology and basic parachute activities should be introduced to the participants:

#1

APERTURE
   The hole in the middle of the parachute which allows air to escape. This enables the parachute to descend slowly and keep the proper shape without bobbing (Popen & Miller, 1967). See illustration #1.

CLOUD
   Participants form an umbrella (see page 9) then allow the parachute to be released. This will form a "cloud" while the participants try to avoid letting the cloud fall on them. See illustration #2.

#2

COUNT-OFF
   Allows you to form groups of individuals who will only respond to the same number called or allows you to form teams consisting of an equal number (or nearly equal number) of team members. For example, a group leader who wanted to form 6 teams (or 6 groups of individuals with

the same number) would ask the participants (say 24 people, to make it come out even) to form a line. The first person in line would start the count by saying or yelling, "One," the next person in line says "2", and so forth until the 4th person is reached, then the 5th person starts the count over by saying "One", the next "2" and so forth on down the line giving you 6 groups or teams of 4 persons each. With this arrangement, for example, only participants with the same number could be directed to react to the group leader's commands.

#3

FORWARD BEND

Participants stand facing the parachute spaced evenly around it. They reach down and grasp the chute's edge with both hands using an overhand grip and bring the parachute up to waist level. Then participants place one foot forward and bend over at the waist while placing their upper bodies over the edge of the parachute with their heads laying on the chute and their arms out to the sides along the parachute's edges prior to executing a new movement (Jacobsen, 1975). See illustration #3.

INFLATION/DEFLATION

After the "forward bend", participants quickly stand up straight, and, making sure they have a tight grip on the chute, throw their arms straight up overhead in unison causing the canopy to rapidly fill with air (inflation). By bending over or stooping down and pulling the parachute back to the floor, the air is allowed to escape (deflation) and the parachute can be easily returned to its initial position, if desired.

#4

UMBRELLA

After you have chosen a group leader, the parachute is spread on the floor as participants face the chute, squat on their knees, and grasp the edge of the parachute with both hands using an overhand grip. When the group leader says, "Go", everyone rapidly stands up and quickly raises the parachute high into the air by throwing their arms straight up over their heads making sure to keep a tight hold as they do so. With the parachute in the resulting dome shape a variety of activities can be performed. See illustration #4.

MUSHROOM

First, an "umbrella" (see above) is formed.
Then everyone quickly takes 4 steps or more into the middle. Have the participants look up inside at the center of the parachute which is forming a "mushroom". See illustration #5 at the top of page 10.

POP THE PARACHUTE

Everyone stands facing the parachute spaced evenly
around it. They reach down and grasp the chute's
edge with both hands using an overhand grip and
bring the chute up to waist or shoulder level. Then,
making sure to keep a tight hold of the chute's edge
with both hands, participants make a vigorous snap-
ping or popping of the canopy. (See illustration
#6 below.) This action is designed to remove
balls or other objects from the surface of the
parachute.

RIPPLES AND WAVES

Everyone stands facing the parachute spaced
evenly around it. They reach down and grasp
the chute's edge with both hands using an overhand grip and bring the chute up to waist or
shoulder level. Participants then make a vigorous shaking or continuous ripple-like (or wave-
like) rolling action which moves the parachute up
and down. This can be a very strenuous arm and
shoulder action, if maintained for prolonged periods.
See illustration #7 below.

RIBS

Parachutes have either nylon cords or double stitched seams extending from the
center hole (aperture) to the perimeter of the parachute. These are evenly
spaced and provide reinforcement for the parachute and a place for individuals
to hold on for the ultimate action desired.

MOUNTAIN (BUBBLE HOUSE)

The parachute is initially raised as high as possible as in "inflation" (see
page 9), or better yet, "mushroom" (also on page 9). Then all the participants
pull the edge of the parachute down to the floor and kneel down to place their
knees on the edge of the chute. This forms a "mountain". (See illustration
#8 at the top of page 11.) An "inner mountain" (cave) is performed by raising
the parachute as in "inflation" or "mushroom" (see page 9) then stepping underneath the parachute or the igloo-like space that is formed, turning completely

10

around to face away from the chute's center and pulling the parachute down over their heads while kneeling down to place their knees on the edge of the
chute. Now the parachute is covering all the
participants and each looks around at all their
friends in the "cave".

#8

BASIC BEGINNING PROCEDURE

This is probably the most basic parachute
preparation procedure that is used prior to
most parachute activities. It was mentioned in
the procedure for "Forward Bend", "Pop The Parachute",
and in "Ripples And Waves". You simply have everyone stand facing the parachute
spaced evenly around it. Then they reach down and grasp the chute's edge with
both hands using an overhand grip and bring the parachute up to the desired
level, usually waist level.

SELECTING APPROPRIATE ACTIVITIES

For each activity presented in this book, the major physical education or recreation objective has been identified. It should be remembered that numerous other
objectives may also be identified. Very few, if any, activity involves only one
physical fitness, perceptual-motor, dance, game, or academic objective. For instance, if your major objective is throwing, the activity also includes upper
body strength, flexibility, balance, agility, as well as, rhythm.

Once a specific objective has been determined, the appropriate activities should
be selected. Use the Table Of Contents to assist you in selecting the activities
that specifically meet your objective(s). And as you make your selections, you
must always remember to match the activity to the ability level of the participants and do not attempt to match the participants to an activity. When selecting an activity, remember that some groups may need help to perform a parachute
activity or the activity may be inappropriate without being modified; for example:

1) Many of our activities are suitable for preschool children if you involve
   parents or aides to help accomplish the selected activity.

2) For some older folks, individuals with certain handicapping conditions, or
   individuals who are just out of shape, an activity may be "medically" too
   active.

3) While physically able, some individuals (that is, individuals who are young
   or mentally retarded) may not be able to understand the "action" of the activity. The complete activity does not have to be mastered on the first
   try. There is nothing wrong with doing a portion of the activity and build-
   ing up slowly in a logical progression.

As a rule of thumb, use your professional instincts and knowledge of your group
in selecting the appropriate activities! This will provide a safe, instructional,
and enjoyable environment for the participants.

PHYSICAL FITNESS ACTIVITIES

Physical fitness is a global term which incorpor-
ates a combination of several components that
can be developed or maintained by parachute activities. The goals for this chapter include the development of muscular strength and endurance, flexibility, and
cardiorespiratory endurance which can be improved by specific parachute activities. Generally all of the following
activities are performed by numerical commands by the the
group leader or an assigned participant to insure that the participants are working together. It is important that all movement be smooth and sustained, that is,
performed without bouncy or jerky motions. Generally, endurance activities should
be only performed a specific number of times based on the populations you are working with and the goals you have developed. Flexibility activities should be gradually increased until each position is held for approximately 10 seconds. The following parachute activities are those which can be utilized to promote physical
fitness.

MUSCULAR STRENGTH AND ENDURANCE ACTIVITIES

The amount of force that a muscle or group
of muscles can exert in one maximum
effort is termed "muscular
strength" while the term "muscular endurance" is defined
as working against moderate
resistance for a prolonged
period. In this section, the
primary goals are to develop
or maintain both muscular strength
and muscular endurance. Some of the
parachute activities which promote muscular strength and endurance include:

THE CLOCK

OBJECTIVES
  Conditioning arms and shoulder girdle and legs.

ACTION
  First, choose someone to sit in the center of the parachute. Remainder of the
  group stand facing the parachute spaced evenly around it. They then squat down

and grasp the parachute's edge with both hands using an overhand grip. While making sure to keep their backs straight, they rise straight up lifting the person on the chute as they do so. Everyone around the chute's edge walks in a circle to the left (counterclockwise) and later to the right (clockwise) as in illustration #1.

#1

TEACHING HINTS

Everyone can lift with just one hand then the other. Try also to raise and lower the parachute to the ankle, knee, waist, and chest level. You can vary the activity by running, galloping, and skipping. Remember to lower the parachute slowly at the end of the activity! For safety, make sure the parachute is strong enough to support someone without pulling apart at the seams as some older or lower quality chutes can do. Also make sure to do everything in unison in order to reduce the strain on any one individual.

MILKSHAKE

OBJECTIVES

Conditioning arms and shoulder girdle.

ACTION

Participants perform the "ripples and waves" action (see page 10). This also can be described as "mixing a milkshake".

TEACHING HINTS

You can vary the tempo and duration of shaking. In addition, the distance between hands can be increased to exercise different portions of the arms and shoulders.

STRETCH A CLOUD

#2

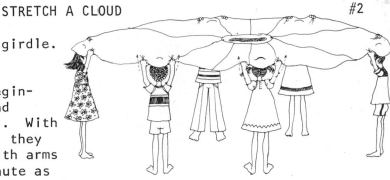

OBJECTIVES

Conditioning arms and shoulder girdle.

ACTION

Everyone initiates the basic beginning procedure (see page 11) and brings the chute to waist level. With their legs and back stationary, they raise the parachute overhead with arms straight and stretch the parachute as far behind their heads as possible as in illustration #2.

TEACHING HINTS

Use a variation with both hands in a palms up grip turning the body so that the back is toward the center of the parachute. You can also vary the distance between their hands.

CIRCLE TUG-A-WAR

#3

OBJECTIVES
  Conditioning arms and shoulder girdle.

ACTION
  Everyone stands with their backs to the
  parachute spaced evenly around it.
  They squat down and reach behind themselves and grasp the chute edge with both
  hands using an underhand grip. They then
  stand up while bringing the chute up to
  waist level. On the signal, "Go", each
  participant leans forward and pulls as hard as possible. See illustration #3.

TEACHING HINTS
  You can vary distance between the grip. Or divide the participants into 2 groups
  and have each group sit on the floor facing each other with the parachute laying between them across a dividing line. On the signal "Go", everyone grabs
  the chute's edge in an overhand grip with both hands and pulls hard to determine which group can pull the other to their side of the line.

BICEP BUILDER

#4

OBJECTIVES
  Conditioning arms and shoulder girdle.

ACTION
  The participants initiate the basic
  beginning procedure (see page 11)
  bringing chute to waist level. They
  stand with one leg forward, plant their
  feet firmly, and lean back with arms
  almost fully extended. On the signal
  "Go", everyone pulls the parachute toward themselves without moving their feet or jerking the
  parachute. See illustration #4.

TEACHING HINTS
  You can vary by counting aloud; the higher the count, the harder the pull.
  Also you may encourage participants to sustain their pull by counting 1001,
  1002, etc.

TRICEP BUILDER

OBJECTIVES
  Conditioning arms and shoulder girdle.

ACTION
  Participants use the same action as in the "Bicep Builder", except that they
  hold the chute with the palms down grip.

TEACHING HINTS
  Try to sustain pull as long as possible. Also you can vary the distance between the hands.

OVERARM PULL

OBJECTIVES
   Conditioning arms and shoulder girdle.

ACTION
   Everyone initiates the basic beginning
   procedure (see page 11) except that
   they cross their right arms over their
   left as they grasp the chute's edge with
   both hands using an overhand grip and
   bring the parachute up to waist level. Then
   have everyone pull for 5 to 10 seconds. See illustration #5.

TEACHING HINTS
   Try this activity with a variety of hand grips (palms up, palms down, left palm
   up, right palm down,and vice versa).

WALKING ON CLOUDS   #6

OBJECTIVES
   Conditioning arms and shoulder girdle.

ACTION
   If they have not already done so, participants remove their shoes and socks (shoes
   are hard on a parachute and stocking feet can
   slip on a nylon chute) and sit facing the parachute spaced evenly around it.
   They reach over and grasp the chute's edge with both hands using an overhand
   grip and bring the chute up to lap or shoulder level and make ripples and waves
   (see page 10) with the canopy. Then the leader chooses one individual to stand
   up and walk/jog, etc., on the top of the parachute while it is rippling and
   waving. See illustration #6.

TEACHING HINTS
   You can vary positions of the body by allowing everyone to kneel, and change
   the distance between grips.

THE CANNON   #7

OBJECTIVES
   Arm and shoulder girdle conditioning.

ACTION
   Everyone initiates the basic beginning procedure (see page 11) bringing the chute up to
   waist or shoulder level. You may place a
   large ball (6 to 10 inch diameter) in the center of the parachute and allow everyone to blast
   it high into the air by lifting their arms up and
   down as quickly as possible. See illustration #7.

TEACHING HINTS
   Vary this activity by reversing hand grips (palms up, down, etc.), and/or by
   counting to a specific number of vigorous preliminary shakes before blasting
   the cannon.

JACK-UP THE CAR

#8

OBJECTIVES
Conditioning abdominal muscles.

ACTION
Everyone sits on the floor with their legs under the parachute. They can perform sit-ups while holding onto the parachute's edge with both hands using an overhand grip. See illustration #8.

TEACHING HINTS
Alternate the participants who go up and down or only let the participants around one-half of the parachute perform the activity while the other half holds tightly to the chute.

ABDOMINAL CURL

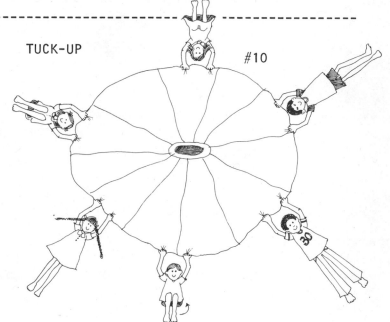

#9

OBJECTIVES
Abdominal conditioning.

ACTION
Everyone sits on the floor facing the chute in the standard bent knee sitting position with folded legs under the parachute. Both hands should firmly grasp the chute's edge using an overhand grip. Without unfolding their legs, have everyone lie back on the floor and then pull themselves up to a sitting position. See illustration #9.

TEACHING HINTS
As a lead-up activity, have everyone lean back in a sitting position and pull themselves up with the chute using an overhand grip to lift only their heads and shoulders off the floor just short of a sit-up position.

TUCK-UP

#10

OBJECTIVES
Abdominal conditioning.

ACTION
Everyone lies on their back with their legs under the parachute spaced evenly around it while grasping the chute's edge with both hands using an overhand grip. Participants curl their knees to their chests and extend legs straight out again to starting position. See illustration #10.

TEACHING HINTS

You can gradually increase the number of repetitions performed by the participants.

SIDE PULLS

#11

OBJECTIVES

Lateral abdominal conditioning.

ACTION

Everyone sits on the floor facing
the chute evenly spaced around it
in the standard bent knee sitting
position with folded legs under the
parachute. Both hands firmly grasp the
chute's edge using an overhand grip. Using
a flexed (bent) arm position, participants pull and twist their trunks to the
left. They repeat the activity several times and then try the activity to the
right. See illustration #11.

TEACHING HINTS

You can hold each position for several seconds, performing each motion slowly
without jerking before returning to the starting position. Another method is
to pull on one side and switch to the other side.

SIDE LEG RAISE

#12

OBJECTIVES

Lateral abdominal conditioning.

ACTION

Everyone lies on the same sides of
their bodies with their feet pointing away from the parachute. With
legs straight, they grasp the chute
with one hand using an overhand grip while
the other hand is stretched out on the floor past their heads under the parachute. Then have everyone slowly raise their top legs while raising the parachute with their hands at the same time and then return to their starting positions. Now you can try the activity on the other side. See illustration #12.

TEACHING HINTS

You can gradually increase the height of the leg that is raised and increase
the time the leg and arm are elevated.

THE SUNRISE

#13

OBJECTIVES

Hands and wrist conditioning.

ACTION

Everyone initiates the basic beginning
procedure (see page 11). Starting
from the parachute's edge they roll up
the chute with both hands until all

participants reach the parachute's center. Then participants slowly unroll the chute while moving backwards. See illustration #13 at the bottom of page 17.

TEACHING HINTS
You can also use teams to see who can reach the center of the parachute first.

HOT TORTILLA

OBJECTIVES
Hand and wrist conditioning.

ACTION
Everyone initiates the basic beginning procedure (see page 11). They then pass the parachute from hand to hand (one hand releasing the chute at a time) around the circle of participants without crossing hands.

TEACHING HINTS
You can vary the direction and speed of the activity by stopping and starting as many times as desirable.

CHEST LIFTER

OBJECTIVES
Conditioning upper back.

ACTION
Participants lie on their stomachs evenly spaced around the chute with feet pointing away from the parachute while keeping their bodies straight. They grasp the parachute's edge with both hands using an overhand grip while sliding backwards until there is some tension. Participants vigorously lift the parachute from the ground with their hands while their heads and chests are still on the ground. Everyone then returns the chute to the ground and repeats the activity.

TEACHING HINTS
Gradually increase the duration of the activity to approximately 10 seconds. To avoid undue back strain, remember not to let anyone arch their backs.

LOWER BACK RAISE

#14

OBJECTIVES
Conditioning lower back.

ACTION
Participants lie on their stomachs with their feet together evenly spaced around the parachute. Their arms are outstretched together on the floor grasping the chute's edge with both hands using an overhand grip. A pillow or rolled up towel is placed under their hips. Participants lift their legs approximately 4 inches and then slowly return them to their starting positions. See illustration #14.

    You may gradually increase the activity to 10 seconds. Remember not to let
    anyone arch their backs because this will put excess stress on their lower
    backs.

HIP RAISE

OBJECTIVES
    Conditioning back.

#15

ACTION
    Have everyone lie on their backs
    evenly spaced around the parachute with their heads
    pointing toward the chute. Their knees are bent and
    their feet are flat on the floor in a comfortable position.
    Arms are straight back beyond their heads with both hands grasp-
    ing the parachute's edge in an underhand grip. Their feet leave the ground
    as their knees and hips tilt forward and momentarily remain in this raised
    position. Then slowly allow them to return to the starting position. See
    illustration #15.

TEACHING HINTS
    Perform each activity with the legs straight and gradually increase duration
    to 5 seconds. Remind everyone to avoid arching their backs. Also you can di-
    vide the class in half so that participants holding one half of the parachute
    perform the activity while the other half holds the parachute taunt.

CRABWALK

OBJECTIVES
    Conditioning arms and shoulder girdle, leg conditioning.

ACTION
    Standing with backs to the parachute evenly spaced around it, everyone bends
    forward reaching backward between their legs to grasp the chute's edge with
    both hands using an underhand grip. The participants then turn to the left
    and walk sideways counterclockwise in a circle and then turn to the right and
    walk sideways clockwise in a circle while on their tip toes.

TEACHING HINTS
    You should gradually increase the number of steps taken whether walking on tip
    toes, or on heels.

SCOOTING

OBJECTIVES
    Leg and abdominal conditioning.

ACTION
    Participants are on the floor facing the parachute evenly spaced around it in
    an extended sitting position (legs straight out in front with the knees bent

and feet flat on the floor in a comfortable position while chute covers knees).
Arms are crossed in front of their chests and chins are held high while grasping the chute's edge on either side of them with their crossed hands using an overhand grip. On command to "scoot" towards chute, participants pull their seats toward their heels by using heel pressure, pulling on the chute's edge, and by slightly lifting their seats. To repeat the procedure, participants extend their legs forward farther into the parachute and roll up the chute's edge.

TEACHING HINTS
You can vary the grip on the parachute and utilize the competition between two teams to see which can reach the center first.

FLEXIBILITY ACTIVITIES

Flexibility is the ability to move the body and its parts through as wide a range of motion as possible without undue strain to the muscles and attachments (Johnson & Nelson, 1979). The goal in this section is to provide activities which can increase the suppleness of the body and enhance flexibility. These kinds of parachute activities include the following:

--   ----

BEND OVER

OBJECTIVES
Lower limb flexibility development.

ACTION
Initiate the basic beginning procedure (see page 11) bringing the chute up to waist level. Without bouncing or bending their knees, everyone bends toward the chute as far as possible while keeping the parachute off the floor. See illustration #1.

#1

TEACHING HINTS
You can vary the position of the participants' feet (apart/together) and gradually hold this position for approximately 10 seconds. Have everyone try standing on one leg and bending, then the other leg, and so forth in an alternate pattern.

STRADDLE BEND

OBJECTIVES
Hip and lower limb flexibility development.

ACTION

Participants sit in a straddle position (seat on the floor with legs straight out to either side to form a "V") facing the parachute evenly spaced around it while grasping the chute's edge with both hands using an overhand grip just above the knees. Have everyone slowly bend their bodies forward to try to touch the parachute with their heads then slowly return to the starting position. See illustration #2.

TEACHING HINTS

Hold position for approximately 10 seconds. You can vary this by having everyone bend over to try and touch their heads to their right legs, then left, etc.

LUNGE

OBJECTIVES
Lower limb flexibility development.

ACTION

Participants stand facing the parachute while evenly spaced around it. They grasp the chute's edge with their left hands using an overhand grip, then lunge forward with their left feet while their right feet remain stationary, and return. Participants switch hands (and feet) and repeat to the right. See illustration #3.

TEACHING HINTS

Participants can step further each time they "lunge" and hold their new positions for approximately 3 seconds.

TOE TOUCH

OBJECTIVES
Lower limb and upper limb flexibility development.

ACTION

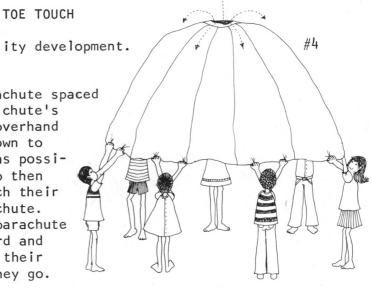

Participants stand facing the parachute spaced evenly around it. They grasp the chute's edge with crossed hands using an overhand grip at waist level. They bend down to touch their toes (or as far down as possible) with their crossed hands grip then immediately come back up to stretch their arms overhead to inflate the parachute. (See illustration #4.) When the parachute is overhead, everyone steps forward and turns to the left while releasing their left hand grips on the chute as they go.

Then, by grasping the parachute again with their left hands on the left sides of their bodies, they end up standing with their backs to the chute. See illustration #5.

TEACHING HINTS
Vary the activity by placing one foot over the other while touching the toes.

BEND AND STRETCH   #6

OBJECTIVES
Lower limb flexibility development.

ACTION
Everyone initiates the basic beginning procedure (see page 11) bringing the chute up to waist level. They bend their knees until squat positions are assumed. Afterwards, participants straighten their legs slowly while holding the parachute close to the floor. See illustration #6.

TEACHING HINTS
You can gradually decrease the distance between the feet by moving them together until the activity is performed with the feet together.

WOOD CHOPPER

OBJECTIVES
Lower and upper limb flexibility development.

ACTION
Everyone initiates the basic beginning procedure (see page 11) bringing the parachute up to waist level. With legs straight and feet approximately 24 to 36 inches apart, they lower the chute down toward their legs as far as possible. Then, without moving their feet, everyone raises the chute above and behind their heads as far as they can.

TEACHING HINTS
You can hold each position approximately 3 seconds before initiating the next action.

SHOULDER ROTATION

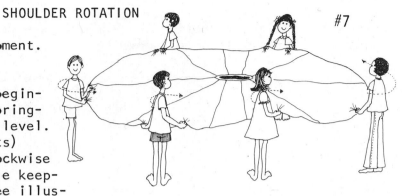

#7

OBJECTIVES
    Upper limb flexibility development.

ACTION
    Everyone initiates the basic begin-
    ning procedure (see page 11) bring-
    ing the parachute up to waist level.
    Everyone rolls (turns or twists)
    their shoulders and trunks clockwise
    and then counterclockwise while keep-
    ing their feet stationary. See illus-
    tration #7.

TEACHING HINTS
    Vary the position of the hands or hold the parachute at shoulder height. You
    can also perform the activity while moving in a circle.

ARM CIRCLES

#8

OBJECTIVES
    Upper limb flexibility development.

ACTION
    Participants stand facing
    the parachute evenly spaced
    around it. They grasp the
    chute's edge with only one
    hand using an overhand grip
    extending sideward at shoulder
    height. Everyone rotates their opposite
    free arms in forward and backward circles.
    They repeat the activity with their other
    arms while the original free arms (hands)
    are now grasping the chute. See illustration #8.

TEACHING HINTS
    Gradually increase size of rotation circles and duration of movement. Also,
    you can perform in a stationary position or while moving in a circle.

TWISTER

#9

OBJECTIVES
    Upper limb flexibility development.

ACTION
    Participants initiate the basic
    beginning procedure (see page 11)
    bringing the parachute up to waist
    level. They rotate their body
    trunks in a half circle to the left
    and then to the right as in doing the "twist" dance.
    See illustration #9.

TEACHING HINTS
Everyone should rotate their trunks slowly and repeat the rotation in the opposite direction. If it helps, move in the opposite direction and then twist.

SIDE STRETCHER #10

OBJECTIVES
Trunk flexibility development.

ACTION
Everyone initiates the basic beginning procedure (see page 11) bringing the parachute up to waist level. Everyone raises the chute overhead and bends to the right, returns to the starting position, and then bends to the left. See illustration #10.

TEACHING HINTS
Hold the bent positions for approximately 3 seconds while bending slowly as far as possible to each side.

BACK STRETCHER

OBJECTIVES
Shoulder flexibility development.

ACTION
Participants stand with their backs to the parachute evenly spaced around it. They squat down to grasp the chute's edge with one hand elevating the chute over their heads and grasping the chute with both hands behind their necks using an underhand grip. Participants stand up and slowly raise their arms as high as possible.

TEACHING HINTS
Participants bend slightly at their waists or you can vary the distance between their hands before repeating the movement.

ROW THE BOAT #11

OBJECTIVES
Shoulder flexibility development.

ACTION
Participants initiate the basic beginning procedure (see page 11) bringing the parachute up to waist level. They move the chute in a circular motion to the right, to the left, then back and forth between participants. They remain stationary (do not move feet) as they do this motion. See illustration #11.

TEACHING HINTS
You can hold the parachute at shoulder height or overhead and repeat the movement.

PULL-BACK

OBJECTIVES
Back flexibility development.

ACTION
Participants initiate the basic beginning procedure (see page 11) bringing the parachute up to shoulder level. Then everyone straightens their
arms to raise the chute overhead
then they pull the chute straight
back beyond their heads while keeping
their arms as straight as possible. See
illustration #12.

TEACHING HINTS
You can vary the distance between the grips or only utilize one hand and repeat
the activity.

SHOULDER SHRUGS

OBJECTIVES
Shoulder flexibility development.

ACTION
Participants initiate the basic beginning procedure (see page 11) bringing the
parachute up to waist level. They slowly raise their shoulders as high as possible (breathing-in helps) and then return to their starting positions.

TEACHING HINTS
You can alternate shrugging of one shoulder then the other while holding the
parachute at waist level. Remember to keep the parachute as taunt as possible.

CARDIORESPIRATORY ENDURANCE ACTIVITIES

Cardiorespiratory endurance is
reflective of an individual
possessing a strong heart,
blood vessels and lungs, and
is generally achieved through
activities such as long distance running, cycling, and
swimming events. The parachute
activities can also be utilized to
develop or maintain cardiorespiratory
endurance. These activities include the following:

WALKING #1

OBJECTIVES
Cardiorespiratory endurance; trunk, and leg endurance development or conditioning.

ACTION
Participants initiate the basic beginning procedure (see page 11) bringing the parachute up to waist level. They turn and walk to the right, then to the left while holding onto the chute with the hand nearest to the parachute. See illustration #1.

TEACHING HINTS
You can vary the speed of the walk from slow to fast, switch directions, and/or hands periodically.

JOGGING #2

OBJECTIVES
Cardiorespiratory endurance; general trunk and leg muscular endurance development or conditioning.

ACTION
Participants initiate the basic beginning procedure (see page 11) bringing the parachute up to waist level. They turn and jog or run to the left (counterclockwise), then to the right (clockwise) while holding onto the chute with only one hand. See illustration #2.

TEACHING HINTS
You should begin the activity at a slow pace. Then gradually increase the duration of the activity to approximately 15 minutes. You can also vary the activity by alternating walking, jogging, and skipping for various durations of time.

GROSS MOTOR SKILLS #3

OBJECTIVES
Cardiorespiratory endurance, coordination, general trunk and leg development.

ACTION
Participants initiate the basic beginning procedure (see page 11) bringing the

26

parachute up to waist level. They turn to the right or left and perform numerous gross motor skills such as running, jumping, skipping, hopping, leaping, galloping, while holding onto the chute with only one hand. See illustration #3 at the bottom of page 26.

TEACHING HINTS
You should begin each activity at a slow pace gradually increasing the duration of the activity to approximately 15 minutes. Also combine several perceptual-motor skills to gradually extend the time of the activity.

RUN IN PLACE

OBJECTIVES
Cardiorespiratory endurance; trunk and leg endurance, arm and shoulder endurance development or conditioning.

ACTION
Participants initiate the basic beginning procedure (see page 11) bringing the parachute up to waist level. Everyone runs in place while alternately lifting their left knees and then their right knees. They can also shake the parachute up and down to make "ripples and waves" (see page 10).

TEACHING HINTS
You should begin at a slow pace for a short duration. Then gradually increase the pace and duration to 15 minutes. Also you can vary the duration of the activity by stopping and starting the activity, and by alternating running and rest periods.

SPRINTS #4

OBJECTIVES
Cardiorespiratory endurance, general leg muscular endurance development or conditioning.

ACTION
Participants stand facing the parachute evenly spaced around it. They reach down and grasp the chute's edge with only one hand in an overhand grip. Then everyone brings the parachute up to any desired level and run in unison as fast as they can to a designated point. (Participants turn their bodies to face the desired direction of movement to allow easier travel.) They switch hands and return to their starting position. See illustration #4.

TEACHING HINTS
You can vary a series of sprints with periods of recovery. For example, a sprint of 20 yards can be followed by a recovery period of walking 20 yards.

OBJECTIVES
   Cardiorespiratory endurance, general
   leg muscular endurance; coordination development or conditioning.

ACTION
   Participants initiate the
   basic beginning procedure
   (see page 11) bringing the
   parachute up to waist level. They
   all jump in different directions on or
   over an imaginary line on the floor. See illustration #5.

TEACHING HINTS
   You can vary the tempo of the jumps and gradually increase the duration of the
   activity. Also vary the movement pattern by placing the feet together and a-
   part as in a "straddle jump".

PERCEPTUAL-MOTOR ACTIVITIES

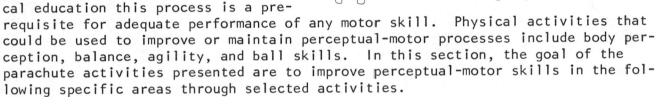

Individuals, of any age, need to take the information gathered from sensory modalities (auditory, visual, haptic, etc.), to organize and make decisions concerning the information, and finally exhibit an overt response based on this information. (This is referred to as the perceptual-motor process.) In physical education this process is a prerequisite for adequate performance of any motor skill. Physical activities that could be used to improve or maintain perceptual-motor processes include body perception, balance, agility, and ball skills. In this section, the goal of the parachute activities presented are to improve perceptual-motor skills in the following specific areas through selected activities.

BODY PERCEPTION

Body perception is the awareness of one's body. It involves the ability to identify body parts, body planes, and body movement; and knowing that one side of the body differs from the other (the difference between the right and left sides); and understanding the spatial relationship of the body to objects in the environment. Parachute activities which can be used to enhance body perception include:

-- ---------

SIMON SAYS

OBJECTIVES
  Identification of body parts and body planes.

ACTION
  Participants initiate the basic beginning procedure (see page 11) bringing the parachute up to waist level. Have everyone place the parachute just below different body parts or planes such as a knee, an arm, front, back, etc. Choose a group leader to give commands for the different body parts. The only time participants should respond to the group leader's command is

when the leader first says "Simon Says". (See illustration #1 at the bottom of page 29.) The group leader may try to trick participants by *not* saying "Simon Says" when a command is given.

TEACHING HINTS

Instead of eliminating participants who are tricked by the group leader, you can develop teams. For a 5 minute period count the number of participants that were tricked by each team and record their scores.

CAN YOU FIND

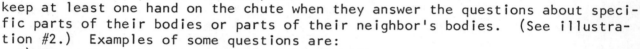

OBJECTIVES

Identification of body planes and body parts in relation to right and left discrimination.

ACTION

Participants initiate the basic beginning procedure (see page 11) bringing the parachute up to waist level. Choose a leader to ask questions about body parts. Participants keep at least one hand on the chute when they answer the questions about specific parts of their bodies or parts of their neighbor's bodies. (See illustration #2.) Examples of some questions are:

1) Can you touch your stomach? Ankles? Elbow?
2) Can you put your hands together? Feet together? Knees together? Thumbs together?
3) Point to a part of the body you hear with. See with. Smell with.
4) Can you touch your right shoulder with your left hand?
5) Can you touch your neighbor's arm?

TEACHING HINTS

The group leader can use flash cards that illustrate the body plane or parts in question on different animals. The participants simply match their body planes or parts with similar ones shown for different animals on each card.

COVER UP

OBJECTIVES

Identification of body parts.

ACTION

Participants take their shoes and socks off (if they have not already done so) and wrap themselves completely or partially in the parachute. See illustration #3.

TEACHING HINTS

You can vary the activity by having everyone wrap only specific body parts.

WHICH WAY ?

#4

OBJECTIVES
Spatial relationship development.

ACTION
First you should choose a group leader. Then participants initiate the basic beginning procedure (see page 11) bringing the parachute up to waist level. They release their right hands from the chute and face in a counterclockwise direction around the chute. The group leader points and calls out the direction (clockwise or counterclockwise) that participants are going to run, walk, etc., while they hold the parachute high above their heads. See illustration #4.

TEACHING HINTS
You can vary the terminology used such as right and left, clockwise and counterclockwise; in and out, inward and outward; inside and outside; and sideways, backward, and forward.

NAME THE PART

#5

OBJECTIVES
Identification of body parts.

ACTION
First choose a group leader and then assign everyone a different number between one and 20 (or more). They make an umbrella (see page 9) with the parachute while the group leader calls out 2 numbers and a particular body part. The 2 players who represent these 2 numbers run under the "umbrella" and point to or touch the specific body parts on themselves or on the other person as commanded by the group leader. (See illustration #5.) The 2 people called must quickly do what they are commanded and return to their places before the chute canopy settles down and touches them.

TEACHING HINTS
Make the activity more complex by being more specific about which body part to touch in terms of which side of the body (that is, right elbow, left knee, etc.).

GHOST CITY

#6

OBJECTIVES
Body awareness development.

ACTION
One participant turns his or her back to the parachute while everyone else hides under it.

(See illustration #6 at the bottom of page 31.) When everyone is quiet, the person outside the chute attempts to identify the ghosts in the city (parachute) by touching and calling out the person's name.

TEACHING HINTS
   Set a time limit and then count the number of ghosts correctly identified. Another technique would be to use 2 parachutes. A member of each parachute team races to identify the members of the other team under their respective parachutes.

THE BLOB

OBJECTIVES
   Identification of body planes and body parts.

ACTION
   First choose a group leader. Everyone else gets under the parachute and lies down (prone) in any comfortable position. The group leader then asks participants to assume different positions by using various body planes and body parts (that is, "Lie down on your back and raise one leg.", etc.) See illustration #7.

TEACHING HINTS
   Make sure there is sufficient space between participants. You can increase the complexity by adding the word "left" or "right" to the group leader's commands.

THE MAN-A-KIN PUZZLE

OBJECTIVES
   Identification of body parts, spatial awareness.

ACTION
   First choose a group leader. Then divide everyone into different numbers or colors. Place cut-outs of the head, arms, hands, feet, legs, and body of a man-a-kin under the parachute. Participants create a mushroom (see page 9) and one of them with a certain number or color walks/runs to the center of the chute and identifies specific body parts called out by the group leader (see illustration #8) and then quickly returns to the edge of the parachute before the chute settles down and touches him or her.

TEACHING HINTS
   You can modify the activity by having each participant whose number or color is called attempt to put the man-a-kin puzzle together in the least amount of time.

FLYING HUMAN

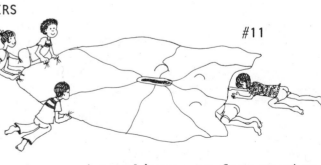

OBJECTIVES
  Identification of body parts or planes

ACTION
  First choose a group leader. Then divide
  the remaining participants up into
  different numbers. Participants
  create an umbrella (see page 9)
  while the group leader calls
  someone's number followed by a
  body part or plane. The person
  called rushes to the center of
  the parachute, jumps into the air
  and while airborne touches a body
  part or plane called by the group
  leader. (See illustration #9.)
  Then he or she quickly returns before the chute
  settles down and touches him or her.

"#5...
TOUCH YOUR
LEFT
THIGH!"

TEACHING HINTS
  You can vary by increasing the number of body parts or planes that must be
  touched while the person is in the air.

CENTIPEDE   #10

OBJECTIVES
  Spatial awareness.

ACTION
  Participants inflate (see page 9) the parachute,
  take 2 steps forward, release the chute, and
  then let it land on themselves. After the
  parachute deflates, all that should be seen are
  the feet of the participants as they walk around.
  (See illustration #10.) Repeat several times.

TEACHING HINTS
  For safety reasons you *must* supervise this activity very closely to avoid collisions.

GOPHERS

OBJECTIVES
  Awareness of the body in relationship to other moving objects.

ACTION
  Direct one half of the participants to face the parachute, kneel, and
  hold the chute taunt close to the floor
  with both hands using an overhand grip.
  The other participants pretend they are gophers and crawl/creep as fast as they
  can underneath the parachute to the other side. (See illustration #11.) Now
  switch places and let the other half try the activity.

Caution must be taken to insure the gophers do not bump into each other. You can vary the activity by selecting 3 gophers then 4, 5, etc.

BALANCE ACTIVITIES

Balance refers to the sense of body position and the ability to maintain (static balance) or regain one's posture or position while moving (dynamic balance). Since balance is an integral component in the development of all perceptual-motor skills, the following parachute activities are designed to develop and improve static and dynamic balance.

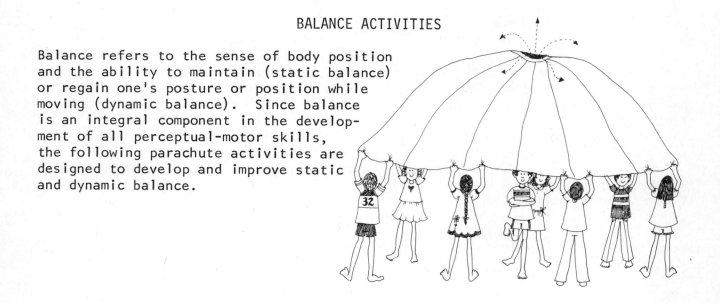

STATIC BALANCE

OBJECTIVES
Stationary balance development.

ACTION
Have everyone initiate the basic beginning procedure (see page 11) bringing the parachute overhead. Next choose a group leader and then call the names of one or more participants and have them perform the static balance activity shown by the leader and return to the edge of the chute before the parachute deflates. Some of the static balance activities may include:
1) Hand knee balance
2) Upright kneeling
3) Straddle balance
4) Front lunge
5) Side lunge
6) Knee balance
7) Balance on one foot (hands on hips)
8) Balance on one foot with the knee raised and arms folded (see illustration above)
9) Front scale
10) Balance on one foot on a 4 inch board (hands on hips)

TEACHING HINTS
You can vary the activity by having everyone close their eyes or do a partner balance such as grasping hands and standing on one foot. Also show pictures of animals, sport heroes, etc., in different balance positions and have the participants imitate them.

DYNAMIC BALANCE

OBJECTIVES
Development of balance while moving.

ACTION

In the same manner as the static balance activities have everyone raise the parachute overhead. Then call one or more of the participant's names and have them perform a balance activity while moving. Some of these activities are:
1) Walking forward between 2 lines
2) Walking backward between 2 lines
3) Walking forward on a one inch wide line
4) Walking backward on a one inch wide line
5) Walking forward on a walking board (see illustration above)
6) Walking backward on a walking board
7) Walking forward on a walking board and returning by walking backward
8) Walking sideways using a crossover step
9) Walking forward while stepping over an object
10) Walking backward while stepping over an object
11) Walking forward on a walking board, picking up an object, and returning by walking backward

TEACHING HINTS

You can vary the activity by performing specific tasks on a line or board on the floor. You can also decrease the time needed to perform each activity.

AGILITY ACTIVITIES

Agility is the ability to switch positions quickly. The following parachute activities can be utilized to develop agility, especially if the group leader stresses that the activity should be performed as fast as possible.

OBJECT GATHERING

OBJECTIVES
Gross agility development in an upright position.

ACTION

First, choose a group leader and then assign each person a different number or color. Place numerous objects (bean bags, deck tennis rings, deflated balls, etc.) on the floor. The participants bend and stretch to make an umbrella (see page 9) with the chute over the objects. The group leader calls 2 names, colors, or numbers and those 2 individuals called go under to see how many objects they can find and carry out before the chute descends and touches them. See illustration #1.

TEACHING HINTS

You can make this activity a game. Divide participants into 2 groups and have each group count off. Call out the names of objects under the parachute, then call out a number representing one participant on each team. These 2 participants attempt to collect as many of these objects as possible and get out before the parachute comes down. A point is awarded for each correct item collected and 2 points are deducted for incorrect items collected. The team with the most points at the end of the game wins.

THE SPEED WAY

OBJECTIVES
Gross agility development in the upright position.

ACTION

First choose a group leader. The remaining participants initiate the basic beginning procedure (see page 11) bringing the parachute up to waist level. They release their left or right hands from the chute's edge and face left or right around the parachute. Participants count off by 4's and take the numbers they call out (see illustration #2). They start running slowly in a circular fashion to the left or right while holding the parachute in one hand at waist level. Group leader calls out numbers between one and 4. Any participant whose number is called immediately releases his or her grip on the chute and runs forward to a new space in front of someone. See illustration #3.

TEACHING HINTS

You can modify the activity by having the participants holding the parachute change directions several times on the signal of the group leader while the individuals whose numbers were called run to the middle of the parachute and then find their homes (original spot) as quickly as possible.

HULA HOOP

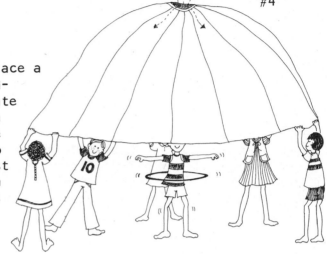

OBJECTIVES
Gross agility development.

ACTION

First choose a group leader. Then place a hula hoop exactly underneath the parachute's aperture. Participants inflate (see page 9) the chute and one person called by the leader rushes under the parachute to the hoop and attempts to twirl the hoop around his or her waist in as many revolutions as possible in "hula" fashion before the chute lands on him or her. See illustration #4.

TEACHING HINTS

You can try this activity using teams.
Place 2 hoops side by side under the parachute's aperture, divide the participants into 2 teams, and number the players with the same numbers on each team. The group leader calls out a number and the player on each team with that number rushes to a hoop and completes as many revolutions ("hulas") around their waists as possible before the chute touches them. (A point is scored for each revolution.) The team with the most revolutions at the end of the game period wins. Another modification is to rotate the hoop or hoops around different body parts, such as, the neck, arms, wrists, or ankles.

OBSTACLES

OBJECTIVES
Gross agility development in an upright position.

ACTION

First choose a group leader. Then place a set of game cones or markers under the parachute in any desired pattern in order to create a "course" to run around or through. Participants then inflate (see page 9) the parachute. The group leader calls upon 2 or 3 people to run the "course" as quickly as possible and then return to home base before the chute settles down and touches them. See illustration #5.

TEACHING HINTS

You can vary the activity by forming 2 teams with one or 2 people from each team running the course. The activity can be even more complex by requiring participants to perform a different motor skill between each course obstacle.

MOTOR SKILL POTPOURRI

OBJECTIVES
Gross agility development in an upright position.

ACTION
First choose a leader. Then everyone initiates the basic beginning procedure (see page 11) bringing the parachute up to waist level. They all release their right or left hands from the chute's edge, turn in unison to the right or left and walk, run, leap, march, jump, hop, slide, gallop, or skip while moving in a circle and while continuously changing directions as commanded by the group leader.

TEACHING HINTS
Caution must be taken not to physically exhaust the participants or perform the activity at a speed that would cause them to bump into each other.

BUBBLE SQUASH

#6

OBJECTIVES
Gross agility development in a crawl/creep position.

ACTION
Participants form a mountain (see pages 10 to 11) with the parachute and quickly crawl from their kneeling positions over the top of the canopy to the center of the chute and then back again as the billowy chute settles to the floor. (See illustration #6.) Each participant must not bump into anyone or must simply stay on the canopy panel in front of them. (As noted before, the parachute canopy is divided up into several panels of cloth formed by seams radiating from the chute's center hole or "aperture".)

TEACHING HINTS
Prevent collisions by requiring participants to move on the parachute panels in front of them and do not allow them to dive or jump into other participants.

TUMBLING

OBJECTIVES
General gross agility development.

ACTION
Choose a group leader who calls out a number of a participant. The participant called runs out under an umbrella (see page 9) that has been formed over a mat, performs a tumbling activity indicated by the group leader, and then runs back to his or her original spot.

TEACHING
Be very careful to select tumbling activities which are appropriate for each participant. Safety must be a major consideration in selecting the activity.

POGO STICK

OBJECTIVES
Gross agility development in an upright position.

ACTION
Choose a group leader who calls out a number representing a participant.
Everyone forms an umbrella (see page 9) with the parachute while the person
whose number was called skips rope or performs jumping jacks as many times as
possible before the parachute canopy lands on him or her or touches the rope
in the case of rope jumping.

TEACHING HINTS
You can increase the complexity of the activity by requiring the rope jumper
to turn the rope counterclockwise or jump (hop) twice before jumping over the
rope. Also, try performing jumping jacks in 6 counts. For example, arms begin at sides of body, then on count of one arms (hands) on hips, count of 2
arms straight out at shoulder height from body sides, count of 3 arms straight
up overhead, on 4 arms back to shoulder height, on 5 arms (hands) on hips again,
and finally on 6 arms down along body sides where they started. The leg action
can also increase the difficulty by straddling (moving out from the sides of the
body as in doing the "splits") on the count of 1, coming together on 2, out
again on 3, back together on 4, and so on.

FLYING PARACHUTE

OBJECTIVES
Gross agility development in an upright
position.

ACTION
Participants stand facing away from
the parachute on one side of it
only while grasping the chute's
edge behind them with one or both hands
(whichever is comfortable) in an overhand
grip. They run to the other side of the gymnasium (or play area) with the parachute flut-
tering behind them. (See illustration #7.) They stop at the other end of the
gymnasium, turn around, get on the other side of the chute (or keep their same
positions), and run back in the same manner.

#7

TEACHING HINTS
You can vary the activity by choosing a group leader who calls out the direction the participants run in .

CRISS-CROSS WALK

OBJECTIVES
Gross agility development in an upright position.

ACTION
First choose a group leader and place a long jump rope under the parachute.
Everyone creates an umbrella (see page 9) with the chute and then when a par-
ticipant's number or color is called out by the group leader, the person called

walks down the rope under the parachute by criss-crossing his or her legs (feet) on either side of the rope. (See illustration #8.) The rope is considered a long knife and should not be stepped on. Participant called must complete the activity in one or both directions before the chute touches him or her as it settles down.

#8

TEACHING HINTS

You can try the activity by criss-crossing the legs (feet) while walking backwards. Also, you can vary the activity by placing 2 ropes under the parachute. For example, divide the participants into 2 equal teams and number each player on both teams with the same number as the other team. Inflate (see page 9) the parachute and the group leader calls out a number that participants on each team represent. These participants whose numbers are called rush out and walk down the rope while criss-crossing their legs along the rope in one direction and then rush back to their positions when finished. The participant who returns first earns one point for his or her team. The team who accumulates the most points at the end of the game wins.

AGILITY HOP

#9

OBJECTIVES

Gross agility development in an upright position.

ACTION

First choose a group leader. Then place 4 or more game cones under the parachute about 5 feet apart in a circle. Participants create an umbrella (see page 9) with the chute and when their particular numbers or colors are called out by the leader, hop a figure 8 pattern around the cones. See illustration #9.

TEACHING HINTS

You may increase the number of cones used and the distance between them. Also try the activity by skipping instead of hopping.

BALL SKILL ACTIVITIES

Ball skills refer to the ability to manipulate, propel or receive objects such as bean bags and balls of various sizes. Ball skills are basic to most games and can be easily incorporated into parachute activities. The following are some examples:

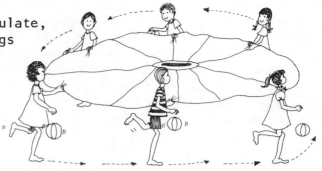

DODGING   #1

OBJECTIVES
Dodging skill development.

ACTION
You should arrange to have 2/3rds of the participants stand facing the parachute spaced evenly around it while grasping the chute's edge at waist level with one or both hands in an overhand grip to form an umbrella (see page 9). The remaining 1/3rd participants get underneath (inside) the parachute. Those on the outside, while still holding the parachute at waist level or higher, use a soft 8½ inch diameter ball to attempt to hit those on the inside. Outside participants must only use their hands to bat or throw the ball at inside participants. They must not kick the ball as this could cause injury depending on the ball's weight. A hit must be below the waist and each inside participant hit joins the outside group. (See illustration #1.) The last remaining participant who is hit wins the game. Repeat the game until all players have had an opportunity to be under the parachute.

TEACHING HINTS
Success in performing this activity is dependent upon enough participants around the parachute to keep it up and the balls under the chute. One or 2 participants can be identified as ball retrievers, if the latter becomes a problem. Another way to modify the activity is to have 1/3rd of the participants as dodgers, 1/3rd as throwers, and 1/3rd as posts to hold the parachute. When someone is hit, he or she becomes a ball retriever.

POPCORN

OBJECTIVES
Hand-eye coordination development.

ACTION
Everyone initiates the basic beginning procedure (see page 11) bringing the parachute up to waist level. Place 3 or more 8½ inch diameter rubber balls (or small bean bags) on and near the center of the parachute. The participants then shake the parachute so the balls bounce like popcorn. See illustration #2 at the top of page 42.

TEACHING HINTS

You can vary the activity by dividing the participants into 2 teams. The participants on one side attempt to shake the balls off the other team's side and vice versa. Keep score on the number of balls that go off each side. Another modification of this activity is to use a variety of ball colors, sizes, and shapes. Participants try to shake one specific type off the chute.

#2

CIRCULAR DRIBBLE

#3

OBJECTIVES

Eye-hand coordination development.

ACTION

You should distribute a ball suitable for dribbling to each participant. Have everyone stand facing the parachute spaced evenly around it. Then have them grasp the chute's edge at waist level with their left hands using an overhand grip. The object is to run in a circular fashion counterclockwise while holding the parachute with the left hand and dribbling the ball with the right hand without losing control of the ball. See illustration #3.

TEACHING HINTS

Since this is the preferred direction for right-handers, it will be more difficult for left-handers. As an equalizer, try dribbling clockwise. The dribble should be started first. Then on signal, all participants start to run. If participant's lose their balls, they must recover them and grasp the parachute at their original places.

ROLLERBALL

#4

OBJECTIVES

Eye-hand coordination development.

ACTION

Participants initiate the basic beginning procedure (see page 11) bringing the parachute up to waist level. Place an 8½ inch diameter ball on the chute and have everyone attempt to roll it around the outer edge of the parachute. This is accomplished by each participant lowering the parachute as the ball nears him or her and raising it as it passes. See illustration #4.

TEACHING HINTS

You can try this activity by placing two 8½ inch diameter balls on the parachute and identifying one ball as the rabbit and the other ball as the hound. The objective is to have the hound chase the rabbit until the 2 balls touch. To make the activity even more complex, try using one or 2 large crab balls (balls that are 4 or more feet in diameter) instead of the smaller ones.

GAMES

Group leaders often find it helpful to
utilize activities with rules and stra-
tegies (games) which emphasize cooperation and competition and also provide an
opportunity to combine physical fitness and perceptual-motor skills.
Cooperation involves everyone working together to achieve a common goal such as
lifting the ball as high as possible into the air from the parachute. Competition
can be emphasized by utilizing team members who cooperate with each other by raising the parachute in unison to throw an opponent's ball off the side of the parachute. Traditionally both cooperation and competition are included in parachute
games and can be utilized to achieve the specific goals of physical fitness and
perceptual-motor skill development. Included in this section are game type activities which can be utilized by group leaders in a variety of settings. The
reader is also referred to the Physical Fitness, Perceptual-Motor, Dance and Academic activities where some selected games have been included.

SNAKE TAG

#1

OBJECTIVES
   Upper body strength, endurance, and coordination development.

ACTION
   Place 4 to 6 long jump ropes without
   handles on the parachute. Divide participants into 2 or more teams spaced
   evenly around the chute. Participants
   make ripples and waves (see page 10) with
   the parachute to try and make one or more of
   the snakes (jump ropes) touch participants on the opposing team. (See illustration #1.) A point is scored against a team whose team member is poisoned
   (touched) by one of the snakes. The team with the lowest score is the winner.

TEACHING HINTS
   Encourage everyone to make ripples and waves (see page 10) for a designated
   time before signaling to stop. Vary by designating different colors for the
   snakes which are more poisonous and award double or triple the numbers of points
   when poisoned (touched) by these snakes. Another modification is designating
   one rope as a cobra. Whoever the cobra touches is eliminated along with his
   or her entire team regardless of the scores of either team.

PARACHUTE KITE RACE

OBJECTIVES
Cardiorespiratory, trunk and leg development.

ACTION

Divide participants into several
teams of 6 to 8 people each.
Then select a team to stand at
one end of the gymnasium or
playground. Team members
should space themselves
evenly around the half of
the chute that is facing
toward the middle of the
playground. With their

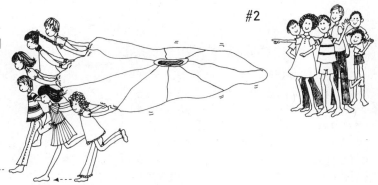

backs to the parachute, team members reach down behind themselves and grasp
the chute's edge with both hands in an underhand grip while bringing the chute
up to waist or shoulder level or overhead. Then, keeping abreast, the team
members run to the other end of the playground and return with the parachute
fluttering behind themselves the entire time. (See illustration #2.) After
team #1 runs, team #2 follows, then team #3, and so forth, until all have run.

TEACHING HINTS

If parachutes are available for each team, have all teams run at one time.
You can also have teams cooperate in a shuttle relay or have each team compete
against one another in a timed race together or one at a time.

CAPTURE THE BACON

OBJECTIVES
Gross agility development in an upright position.

ACTION

Assign the same number to members of both teams
and place a bean bag under the parachute's
aperture. As the participants inflate (see page 9) the parachute,
call a number. Those participants
on each team who represent the number called run under the chute and
try to capture the bacon (bean bag) and
return to their spots before being tagged by the descending parachute. Award
one point to the team whose participant
captures the bacon without being tagged
by the chute or to the team whose player

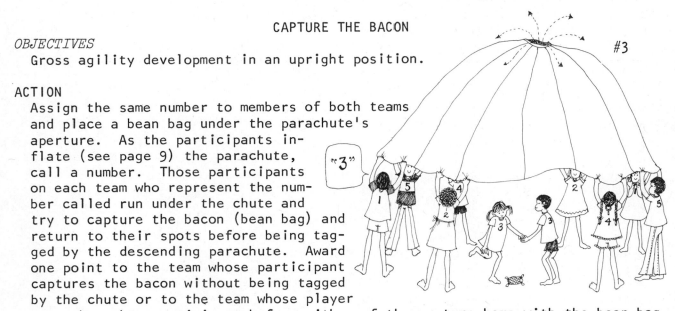

tags the other participant before either of them return home with the bean bag.
See illustration #3.

TEACHING HINTS

You can call 2 or more numbers to capture the bacon. Have everyone run, jump,
hop, etc., to capture the bacon. Place the bacon in a 2 foot diameter circle
that is designated a poison area. If a team's player is tagged by the descending chute while in the poison circle, the opposing team is automatically awarded one point.

POTPOURRI

OBJECTIVES
Ball skill (bouncing) development. (Objective depends on activity selected.)

ACTION

Divide the group into 2, 3 or 4 teams and assign the same numbers to members of each team. Then designate a task (that is, bounce the ball 10 times, etc.). Everyone should initiate the basic beginning procedure (see page 11) bringing the parachute up to waist level. You (or a group leader) call a number and describe a specific task to be performed. Participants on each team who represent the number called, leave their places around the parachute and perform the described task in the activity area under the parachute in a circle on the floor while the other participants make ripples and waves (see page 10). (See illustration #4.) Upon task completion, participants return to their spots on the chute. The first team to complete all the assigned tasks, is the winner.

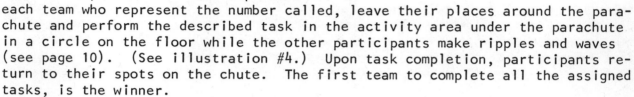

TEACHING HINTS

You can vary the task to include some of the following activities or create others:
1) Perform 10 push-ups.
2) Crawl to the opposite end of the activity area.
3) Roll over 3 times.
4) Hop around the inside of a circle.

PONY EXPRESS

OBJECTIVES

Gross agility development in an upright position.

ACTION

Pair off everyone with one participant designated as the horse and the other the rider. The horses initiate the basic beginning procedure (see page 11) bringing the parachute up to waist level while spreading their legs out to either side in a straddle position. The riders assume a squatting position under the parachute facing their horses. On command, the riders crawl between the legs of their horses and run as fast as they can in a clockwise direction once around the chute and back to their horses. (See illustration #5.) At the same time, the horses make a mountain (see pages 10 to 11) and assume an all 4's position while holding onto the edge of the parachute with their hands instead of their knees as the mountain exercise normally requires. Riders who return to their horses and mount them first, win. (See illustration #6.) Repeat with horse and rider switching positions.

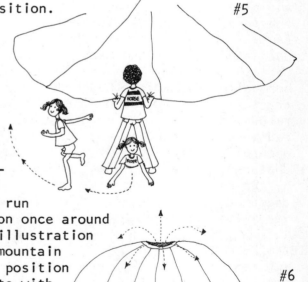

TEACHING HINTS

Caution must be taken to insure that riders do not bump into one another when running around the parachute. You can vary the activity by allowing the horses to gallop, skip, etc.

NAME CHANGE

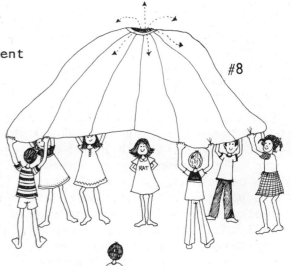

OBJECTIVES

Gross agility development in an upright position.

ACTION

Everyone initiates the basic beginning procedure (see page 11) bring the parachute up overhead. While this is being done, select someone to be "it" and stand underneath the parachute's center. Then call the names of 2 participants who attempt to change places with each other by going around the parachute before being tagged by "it". (See illustration #7.) If "it" is successful, the tagged participant becomes "it" and the game is repeated. If "it" cannot tag someone after 3 tries, designate another individual.

TEACHING HINTS

You can vary the activity by calling the names of more than 2 participants or specify which participant performs what activity. For example, one participant runs while the other skips, etc.

CAT AND RAT

OBJECTIVES

Cardiorespiratory and gross agility development in an upright position.

ACTION

Participants initiate the basic beginning procedure (see page 11) bringing the parachute up overhead. Select one participant to be the cat and one to be the rat. The cat is outside the parachute circle while the rat is inside under the parachute. (See illustration #8.) The following conversation takes place:

   The cat: "I am the cat."
   The rat: "I am the rat."
   The cat: "I will catch you!"
   The rat: "No you can't!"

The cat then chases the rat attempting to tag it. Everyone holding the parachute protects the rat by letting it enter and leave the area under the parachute. At the same time, they try to keep the cat outside the parachute area by using their bodies to block the cat's entry. When the cat tags the rat, the cat becomes the rat and another participant is called upon to be the cat.

You can vary the activity by utilizing 2 cats and 2 rats.

BIRDS, BEASTS, AND FISH

OBJECTIVES
Gross agility development in an upright position.

#9

ACTION
Everyone should count-off (see pages 8 to 9) by 3's. All number one's are Birds, all number 2's are Beasts, and all number 3's are Fish. When the participants inflate (see page 9) the parachute, call out "Birds", "Beasts", or "Fish". All those whose number represents the name called, run under the parachute and change places with one another before the chute settles down and touches them. (See illustration #9.) Repeat, calling another name or combination of names.

TEACHING HINTS
When the participants comprehend changing places with someone else, make the game more interesting by having 3 extra people representing one bird, one fish and one beast stand under the chute. These 3 have no positions around the parachute's edge so there will be 3 people without places to fill at all times. These 3 try to find a position left vacant around the chute when their animal name is called.

GRAND PRIX

OBJECTIVES
Cardiorespiratory, and gross agility (running) development.

ACTION
First choose a group leader. With everyone standing around the parachute, have them count-off (see pages 8 to 9) to form groups of 4 or 5 participants. All participants in each group with the same number are given the same name of a car. The group leader starts the race by calling one of the car names. At the same time, everyone inflates (see page 9) the parachute. All those specific participants representing the car called run around the parachute counterclockwise back into their original positions (garages) and then run under the inflated parachute to the center of the circle to tag the group leader standing there. The group leader represents the finish line. The first one to reach the center to tag the leader wins. The group leader then calls another car name to start the next race. Only cars with the same car name called will race. When the winners of each car type are evident, a final race is held to determine the champion.

TEACHING HINTS
You can vary the activity by using walking or emphasing how slowly participants can walk around the parachute (this is good for slower participants). Also you may utilize jumping, hopping, skipping, etc., around the parachute circle.

PARACHUTE GOLF

#10

OBJECTIVES
   Upper body strength and eye-hand coordination development.

ACTION
   Everyone initiates the basic beginning procedure (see page 11) bringing the parachute up to waist level. Place 3 plastic balls of one color that represent one team and 3 balls of another color that represent the other team on the chute. Make sure the balls are small enough to pass through the parachute's aperture. Each team tries to shake their colored balls through the aperture and keep the other team from doing the same with their 3 colored balls. (See illustration #10.) Score one point for each ball which passes through the aperture.

TEACHING HINTS
   Repeat the game by having everyone try to shake (bounce) their opponent's balls off the parachute's sides (not through the aperture). Or use 5 or 6 balls for each team. If a ball goes in the rough (over the parachute's sides), place it back on the chute and penalize the ball's team one point for losing the ball in the rough.

PARASCOOTER

OBJECTIVES
   Upper body and abdominal strength development.

ACTION
   Participants face the parachute evenly spaced around it in comfortable sitting positions on the scooters while grasping the chute with both hands in an overhand grip. On a signal have participants on one side of the chute lean back and pull while the other side simply sits and holds on while riding the pull of the parachute. The motion is then reversed by having the pulling side ride this time and the riding side pull. After each side or team has had a chance to be pulled, both sides try to pull each other at once across a designated line as in tug-o-war. (See illustration #11.) Participants must stay on their scooters and are not allowed to touch the floor with their feet, hands, or any other part of their bodies in order to get pulling leverage.

TEACHING HINTS
   You can have everyone reverse their pulling-riding roles in a slow to faster pattern. Also, vary the activity by having participants use other body support positions on the scooters besides sitting. However, do not let them stand on the scooters because this would obviously be very dangerous.

PARACHUTE VOLLEY

OBJECTIVES
   Upper body strength, gross agility in an upright position,and eye-hand coordination development.

ACTION

Divide the participants into 2 groups with one chute per group. Each group initiates the basic beginning procedure (see page 11) with their own parachutes and brings them up to waist level. One group tosses (bounces) a ball from their chute to the other group's parachute and back again. (See illustration #12.) A record is kept to record the number of catches for each group in a specified time period.

TEACHING HINTS

You can vary the activity by utilizing teams and awarding points to each team by:
1) Volleying for greatest height.
2) Volleying for greatest distance.
3) Number of consecutive volleys.
4) Number of baskets scored.
5) Number of targets hit.

MISSLE LAUNCH

OBJECTIVES
Ball skill (throwing, bouncing) development.

ACTION

Everyone lines up and counts-off (see pages 8 to 9) by 4's (or by 3's, 5's, etc., whatever works best for the number of participants available). On a designated signal, participants form an umbrella (see page 9) with a parachute while at the same time a team or group number is called. In the meantime, make sure there are four $8\frac{1}{2}$ inch diameter balls (one ball for each of the 4 groups) underneath the chute's aperture. Team members, representing the number called, run to the balls and attempt to bounce them off the floor and in doing so, propel the balls through the parachute's aperture before the chute deflates. See illustration #13.

TEACHING HINTS

You can have team members who bounce the balls go and retrieve the balls before returning to their places around the parachute. Also you may vary the activity by placing a tire or hoop in the center below the chute's aperture to hold the balls in place. When the activity begins, the tire or hoop will be an obstacle making the correct launching more complex.

THE CHASE

OBJECTIVES
Gross agility in an upright position and ball skill (throwing) development.

ACTION

First choose a participant to be "it".
The rest of the participants initiate
the basic beginning procedure (see
page 11) bringing the parachute up
to waist level. The participant
who is "it", stands outside the
parachute circle holding a sponge
ball. "It" walks around the circle
while the parachute is being inflated (see page
9) making ripples and waves (see page 10) and
places the ball behind one of the participants.
(See illustration #14.) The participant who has the
ball placed behind him or her picks the ball up
and chases "it" around the parachute
circle clockwise while trying to hit
"it" with the sponge ball before
"it" reaches the recently vacated
spot and grasps the parachute with
both hands using an overhand grip.
(See illustration #15.) The game
continues as the new "it" places
the sponge ball behind a new participant.

#14

#15

TEACHING HINTS

Also you can have the participants hop, gallop,
skip, etc., around the parachute. Another way
to vary the activity is to allow "it" to drop a flag behind one of the players
and have the chaser tag "it" before "it" reaches the chaser's vacant spot on
the parachute.

DANCE

Dance is generally defined as a
rhythmic movement of the body which
provides an opportunity for creative and interpretive communica-
tion. It has been an integral
part of man's history. Even as
far back as prehistoric times,
early man was believed to have
joined hands and repeated rhythmical patterns to the gods. Today
people in every country participate in dance.

There are basically 4 classifications of dance that will be discussed in this
section. These are: fundamental rhythms, creative rhythms (sometimes called
"problem solving"), singing rhythms, and folk dance (Gallahue & Meadows, 1974).
There are numerous dances within each classification that can be incorporated
into parachute activities.

The goals of teaching dance activities to your group can be divided into 4 broad
categories:
   1) SKILL - Develop the ability to perform a broad range of steps and dances;
       to dance rhythmically with appropriate timing, phrasing, and patterns;
       and develop a minimal skill to enjoy dance activities.
   2) SOCIAL - Learn cooperation and accept the responsibility of playing a speci-
       fic role; get acquainted with others; and have fun.
   3) EMOTIONAL - Joy of moving and creating.
   4) AESTHETICS - Develop the ability to perform dance activities because of the
       nature of beauty and judgements concerning beauty which are related to
       these activities.

FUNDAMENTAL RHYTHMS

Fundamental rhythms involve the use of numerous movements to develop a basic a-
wareness of the elements of rhythm and space. The following basic elements of
rhythm include examples of how you can explore each through parachute activities
with your class:

UNDERLYING BEAT
   The continuous sound that is heard during any rhythmical sequence. The underlying beat of the music may be explored using the following movement sequence:

1) Listen to the music, try to feel the sequence of pulse beats.
2) Move the head to the beat.
3) Move the hands to make small waves with the parachute.
4) Walk in place to each beat.
5) Move forward, backward, and sideward to the beat.
6) Change the tempo of the music and repeat all actions.

ACCENT

The emphasis (force) in any one beat. It is usually the first beat in a measure. Identifying and moving to the strong beat of music offers numerous parachute activities. Beginning with 4/4 meter allows participants the easiest mode for movement. The activities emphasize the accent elements of movement:
   1) Make strong hand movements on the first beat and light movements on the other beats.
   2) Stamp loudly on the first beat, walk in place softly on the other beats.
   3) Walk forward with long steps on the first beat and short steps on the other beats.
   4) Moving forward, backward, or sideward; change direction on the heavy beat.
   5) Use various locomotor steps to find the first beat.
   6) Accent the first beat of various meters including 2/4, 3/4, 6/8.

PHRASING

A musical phrase is similiar to a language sentence or combination of language sentences. It is at least 2 measures long and contains a continuous thematic sequence. Listen to the music to identify various parts. You should note phrases as they are played. While holding the parachute in one hand, participants can try the following activities:
   1) Move the arm and chute up at the beginning of each phrase.
   2) Walking around the chute, change direction at each new phrase.
   3) Using any non-locomotor movement in place or combined with a locomotor movement, change movement with each new phrase.

RHYTHMIC PATTERN

The grouping of sounds or beats that are related to the underlying beat. Movement to rhythmic patterns is more difficult than response to underlying beat, accents, or phrasing, however, some activities involving response to name patterns or nursery rhymes may provide a satisfying experience. The following sequence consists of suggested ideas that may be used in developing rhythmic patterns that use the names of the participants.
   1) Clap the rhythmic pattern of each name.
   2) Move some other part of the body to the pattern.
   3) Decide which locomotor steps best fit the rhythmic pattern.
   4) Try the locomotor step pattern with the chute.
   5) Repeat the pattern several times while changing direction, levels, or movement intensity.
   6) Put 2 or more name rhythmic patterns in sequential order.

SPACE ELEMENTS

There are also basic space elements that are incorporated into fundamental rhythms. These are direction, level, and space patterns (Schurr, 1980). Direction involves the line of movement taken. It could be forwards, backwards, sideways, diagonally, up, down, etc. The levels involve the location of the body as it relates to high, medium, and low (such as standing, bent over, sitting, etc.) during an activity. The space pattern involves the extension of direction by making specific designs with the moving body during an activity. It could be a square, triangle, circle, straight line, etc.

There are numerous locomotor and nonlocomotor movements that you can incorporate in parachute activities to develop an understanding of the elements of rhythm and space.

LOCOMOTOR MOVEMENT

A walk, a run, a leap, a jump, and a hop are all ways of moving the body through space to an even beat. You can explore many variations by holding the parachute in either one hand or 2 hands that include the following:

DIRECTIONS

Move forward, backward, sideward, up, and down.

SPEED

Move slowly, fast, accelerating, and decelerating.

COMBINING STEPS

Combine a walk and run, a jump and hop, a run and leap, combine steps using a different number, that is, 2 runs and 4 jumps; 4 walks and 2 leaps; 4 walks, 4 runs, and 4 leaps.

FORCE

Move with heavy steps, light, springy, or skimming.

Skipping, sliding, and galloping combine 2 locomotor movements. The skip consists of a walk and a hop. The gallop consists of a walk and a leap. And the slide consists of a walk and a leap sideward. The beat is uneven. Variations may be developed by changing the direction, level, speed, or force of the movement. The following sequence is an example of what may be done to any 4 beat music.
1) Grasp the parachute with 2 hands and skip 8 steps forward while lifting the parachute into a mushroom (see page 9).
2) Skip 8 steps backward while lowering the parachute.
3) Slide 4 slides to the right.
4) Slide 4 slides to the left.

NONLOCOMOTOR MOVEMENT

Body movements such as bend, stretch, and swing, which may be done in place, are called nonlocomotor movements. Combining 2 nonlocomotor movements offers special opportunities for parachute activities. Three possible combinations are suggested here:

BENDING AND STRETCHING

While grasping the parachute in various ways while facing backwards and sidewards try the following activities:
1) Body Parts - Bend and stretch arms, legs, neck, and trunk.
2) Levels - Change body levels from high to low while bending and stretching.
3) Speed - Bend and stretch very slowly, rapidly, and change from slow to fast.

4) Force - Vary the amount of force used in bending and stretching.

SWINGING AND SWAYING
1) Body Parts - Swing or sway one arm, both arms, the trunk, one leg forward and back or sidewards.
2) Level - Swing or sway in an upright position.
3) Speed - Swing or sway very slowly, rapidly, change from slow to fast.
4) Imaginative - Swing or sway like an elephant's trunk, a flying trapeze.
5) Combinations - Combine swinging movements with swaying movements. While facing the chute begin with large arm swings. Gradually diminish the movement until just the feet are initiating the swaying movement side to side.

TWISTING AND TURNING
Twisting consists of a rotation of a part of the body around a long axis. In "turning", the whole body rotates. A twist is executed either clockwise or counterclockwise. While holding the parachute in various ways try the following:
1) Twist various body parts: a) arms at shoulders, elbows, wrist; b) legs at hips, knees, and ankles; c) trunk to the left and around to the right; and d) neck to the left and right.
2) Change speed from slow to fast in twisting or turning.
3) Move to high, medium and low levels while twisting various body parts.
4) Combine twisting and turning movements. For example: face parachute, hold it with 2 hands, lift parachute above the heads, twist right knee in and out twice, repeat action with left knee, then drop the chute, and make a complete turn around, catch parachute on its' way down.
5) Move around, and in and out of the parachute while combining twisting and turning with locomotor steps.

CREATIVE RHYTHMS

Creative rhythm is an extension of rhythmic fundamentals which allows for the expression of emotions and feelings. Individuals could be asked to: a) represent vehicles, b) assume the role of an animal, c) make human non-speech sounds, d) pantomime various objects, or e) express moods. Examples or representative activities are:
1) Represent vehicles: cars, motor bikes, trains, airplanes, missles, etc.
2) Assume the role of an animal: horses, buffalo, cats, lions, apes, dogs, etc. Animal sounds can be added.
3) Make human non-speech sounds: groaning, sniffing, laughing, shouting, yawning, snoring, sighing, etc.
4) Pantomime various objects: Movements of machines, balls, hoops, wands, etc.
5) Express moods: excitement, depression, impulsive, joy, reflective, sadness, happiness, thoughtfulness, rage, etc.

A group leader can easily introduce this form of dance in parachute activities. Just have the participants form an umbrella while one or more participants run underneath to the center of the parachute and perform a creative activity before the chute lands on them.

SINGING RHYTHMS

Singing rhythms require individuals to perform specific movements in addition to singing. This develops the sense of rhythmic movement. You can adapt almost any action song into a parachute activity. Note that all of the parachute activities listed in this Dance section are examples of singing rhythms modified for use with a parachute.

Many or some of the following rhythmic singing activities will no doubt be unfamiliar to you and your group. Do not worry about it! Simply have everyone say the words out loud. The very fact that they say the words out loud in unison will establish its own rhythmic beat. This is called "chanting". In order to guide the cadence or beat of the "chanting", be sure and have everyone say the words with you and follow your lead. (You could even stomp your feet to each word, part-word, every other word, etc.) After several run-throughs, you will find that the chanting experience will create its own beat that will be best for the particular activities suggested.

WALK WITH ME

OBJECTIVES
Coordinate walking skills to rhythm.

ACTION
Everyone initiates the basic beginning procedure (see page 11) bringing the parachute up to waist level. Participants release their right hands, turn to the right and walk counterclockwise singing or chanting the words:

Will you come and walk with me
Will you come and walk with me,
Will you come and walk with me
All around the room.

TEACHING HINTS
Continuously change the action word from walking, to jumping, hopping, running, galloping, etc.

TEN LITTLE INDIANS

OBJECTIVES
Coordinate lower body gross agility
skill to rhythm.

ACTION
Everyone counts-off by
10's (see pages 8 to 9)
and initiates the basic
beginning procedure (see
page 11) bringing the
parachute up to shoulder
level. Then they release
their left hands, turn to the
left and walk clockwise around the
parachute while shaking it (ripples

and waves, see page 10) with their right hands. When a participant's number is sung, he or she moves past the participant in front of him or her. (See illustration #1 at the bottom of page 56.) In the 2nd verse, change the direction and perform the same activity.

Verse 1, sing or chant: 1 little, 2 little, 3 little Indians,
4 little, 5 little, 6 little Indians,
7 little, 8 little, 9 little Indians,
10 little Indian bodys.

Verse 2, sing or chant: 10 little, 9 little, 8 little Indians,
7 little, 6 little, 5 little Indians,
4 little, 3 little, 2 little Indians,
1 little Indian boy.

TEACHING HINTS
You can use a variety of perceptual-motor skills. To make the activity a little more complex, balls could also be placed on the parachute(s). Participants attempt to keep the balls on the parachute while performing the activities.

FIVE LITTLE CHICKADEES

OBJECTIVES
General gross agility development to rhythm.

ACTION
Everyone initiates the basic beginning procedure (see page 11), except for 5 chickadees (participants numbered one to 5) who sit under the parachute at the aperture. The parachute is inflated (see page 9) and the participants around the parachute release their left hands, turn to the left and begin to walk clockwise and sing or chant. On the word, "One flew away", the first chickadee jumps up, joins the others holding the parachute and joins in singing the chorus. This action is repeated until all 5 little chickadees join the participants holding the parachute.

Verse 1, sing or chant: 5 little chickadees, sitting near the door,
one flew away, and then there were 4.

Verse 2, sing or chant: 4 little chickadees, sitting in a tree,
one flew away, and then there were 3.

Verse 3, sing or chant: 3 little chickadees, looking at you,
one flew away, and then there were 2.

Verse 4, sing or chant: 2 little chickadees, sitting in the sun,
one flew away, and then there was one.

Verse 5, sing or chant: One little chickadee, left all alone,
one flew away, and then there was none.

Chorus, sing or chant: Chickadee, chickadee, happy and gay,
Chickadee, chickadee, fly, fly away.

TEACHING HINTS
Try performing other perceptual-motor skills such as hopping, galloping, or skipping. The number of chickadees could also be increased to give more participants an

opportunity to participate. In addition, try counting from 5 backwards to one in the verses, thereby bringing the chickadees back home one by one to their nest (center of the parachute).

MUFFIN MAN

OBJECTIVES
Coordinate lower body agility skill (walking and skipping) to rhythm.

ACTION
Everyone initiates the basic beginning procedure (see page 11) bringing the parachute up to waist level. They release their left hands, turn left, and skip clockwise while singing and making ripples and waves (see page 10) with the chute. One participant (called the "Muffin Man") stands outside the circle. At the beginning of verse 2, everyone holding the parachute stops and inflates it (see page 9) while the "Muffin Man" selects a partner from among them. Then both the "Muffin Man" and selected partner rush underneath the chute while hold-ing hands and skip counterclockwise once around the inside of the parachute circle (being careful not to let the chute descend on them), then run outside of the circle of participants to where they both started.

For verse 3, the 2 participants each select and perform the activity when the parachute is elevated, and so on. Keep singing and performing the activity un-til the parachute cannot be correctly inflated because of the lack of partici-pants holding the chute.

Verse 1, sing or chant: Oh, have you seen the muffin man, the muffin man, the muffin man, Oh, have you seen the muffin man, who lives in Drury Lane?

Verse 2, sing or chant: Oh, yes, we've seen the muffin man, the muffin man, the muffin man, Oh, yes, we've seen the muffin man, who lives in Drury Lane.

Verse 3, sing or chant: 2 have seen the muffin man, the muffin man, the muffin man, Oh, yes, 2 have seen the muffin man, who lives in Drury Lane.

Verse 4, sing or chant: 4 have seen the muffin man, the muffin man, the muffin man, Oh, yes, 4 have seen the muffin man, who lives in Drury Lane.

Verse 5, sing or chant: 8 have seen the muffin man, the muffin man, the muffin man, Oh, yes, 8 have seen the muffin man, who lives in Drury Lane.

TEACHING HINTS
Make sure that participants choose partners who are located at different sec-tions around the parachute so that the chute can be kept in the air as long as possible. Also, vary the type of gross agility skills the participants perform.

OLD KING COLE

OBJECTIVES
Coordinate mimicry skills to rhythm.

ACTION

Participants initiate the basic beginning procedure (see page 11) bringing the parachute up to waist level. They release their left hands, face clockwise and begin to walk. One participant, who represents "King Cole", stands on the outside of the circle. On the first mention of the word "And", the participants stop and inflate (see page 9) the parachute and the King runs underneath the chute to the center. Then, the King points to a participant to bring his pipe. On the 2nd mention of the word "And", he points to a participant to bring his bowl. On the 3rd mention of the word "And", he points to 3 participants to come and be his fiddlers. For the rest of the song or chant the King and his helpers dance around underneath the chute or act out their parts. Afterwards, choose a new King and repeat the activity.

Sing or chant: Old King Cole was a merry old soul
                  And a merry old soul was he,
                  He called for his pipe,
                  And he called for his bowl, And
                  He called for his fiddlers 3.
                  And he called for his fiddlers 3.
                  And he called for his fiddlers 3.
                  Every fiddler had a very fine fiddle,
                  A very fine fiddle had he,
                  And we'll all fiddle for Old King Cole
                  And be as merry as he.

TEACHING HINTS

Try to rotate the participants selected. Many times only a select few are chosen. If this becomes a problem, you should select the pipe carrier, bowl carrier, and fiddlers before the parachute is inflated. The participants around the chute must make sure the parachute does not touch the King and his helpers.

BINGO

OBJECTIVES
Rhythmical development of walking skills.

ACTION
Everyone counts-off by 2's (see pages 8 to 9). Then they initiate the basic beginning procedure (see page 11) bringing the parachute up to waist level. They release their right hands, turn right and walk counterclockwise while making ripples and waves (see page 10). On the singing or chanting of the letter "B", the participants who represent the number one move clockwise past one participant. On the letter "O", the participants who represent the number 2, move counter clockwise past one participant. (See illustration #2.) On the chanting of letters "I", "N", and "G" the participants stay in their spots.

Verse 1, sing or chant: A big black dog sat on the back porch
                          And Bingo was his name.

Verse 2, sing or chant: A big black dog sat on the back porch
                          And Bingo was his name.

Verse 3, sing or chant: B-I-N-G-O, B-I-N-G-O, B-I-N-G-O,
                          And Bingo was his name.

                     B-I-N-G-O

TEACHING HINTS
  Try different gross motor skills and have participants who represent a "B" or
  "O" move past 2 or more participants when "their" letter is sung or chanted.

OH, WHERE HAS MY LITTLE DOG GONE

OBJECTIVES
  Coordinate upper body gross agility skill to rhythm.

ACTION
  Everyone initiates the basic beginning procedure (see page 11) bringing the
  parachute up to waist level. They then release their right hands, turn right
  and walk counterclockwise while singing or chanting. One participant, representing the dog owner, walks clockwise outside the parachute circle looking toward the chute and moving his or her head from side to side looking for the dog.
  At the end of the song or chant, the participants around the chute stop and inflate (see page 9) the parachute. At this time, any participant around the parachute who is in front of the dog owner is identified as the "dog" and runs in
  and out of the trees (participants around the chute) while being chased by the
  dog owner until the parachute comes down. If the owner catches the dog before
  the parachute settles down and touches the owner, the entire activity is repeated again so that a new dog is selected. If the dog is not caught, the dog becomes the dog owner.

  Sing or chant: Oh where, Oh where has my little dog gone
                   Oh where, Oh where can he be?
                   With his tail cut short, and his ears cut long
                   Oh where, Oh where can he be?

TEACHING HINTS
  If the participant who represents the dog seems to be continuously winning, you
  can modify the activity to slow him or her down.

POP GOES THE WEASEL

#3

OBJECTIVES
  Coordinate lower limb gross agility skills to
  rhythm.

ACTION
  Everyone initiates the basic beginning
  procedure (see page 11) bringing the
  parachute up to waist level. Two participants are selected to squat down
  together and form a bench. Two others are
  selected as a monkey and a weasel. All
  participants begin to sing or chant and
  on the word "pop", an umbrella (see page 9)
  is made and the 2 selected "benches" run
  out to form a bench, the weasel runs out, and

60

the monkey runs out to chase the weasel around the bench for the remainder of the song (chant). (See illustration #3 at the bottom of page 60.) Choose 4 new participants and repeat the activity.

Verse 1, sing or chant: All around the cobbler's bench
The monkey chased the weasel,
The monkey thought 'twas all in fun,
Pop! goes the weasel.

Verse 2, sing or chant: A penny for a spool of thread,
A penny for a needle,
That's the way the monkey goes,
Pop! goes the weasel.

TEACHING HINTS
You can vary the perceptual-motor skills performed by the weasel and monkey.

ITISKIT, ITASKIT

OBJECTIVES
Coordinate upper body agility development to rhythm.

ACTION
All participants initiate the basic beginning procedure (see page 11) bringing the parachute up to shoulder level. Everyone makes ripples and waves (see page 10) while one participant who is "It" walks around the parachute circle holding a bean bag. On the sung or chanted words of "...it is you", "It" drops the bean bag behind the nearest participant who is shaking the parachute. This "nearest participant" picks up the bean bag and must chase "It" around the parachute once while trying to tag him or her. When the chase begins, the parachute is inflated (see page 9) and after once around the chute, "It" must go through the spot (doorway) formerly occupied by the chaser on the parachute and run to the center underneath the chute before he or she is tagged. If "It" reaches the center of the parachute before being tagged by the chaser or touched by the descending chute, "It" is "home free" and repeats the entire activity as "It" again with a new chaser. If "It" is tagged by the chaser or touched by the falling parachute before reaching the chute's center, "It" then takes the chaser's place and the chaser becomes the new "It".

Sing or chant: Itiskit, itaskit
A green and yellow basket
I wrote a letter to my love
And on the way I dropped it
I dropped it, I dropped it
One of you has picked it up
And put it in your pocket
It isn't you, it isn't you,
It isn't you, it is YOU!

TEACHING HINTS
As a variation, "It" can remain "It" by running around inside the parachute circle until he or she is tagged. Also, the bean bag can be replaced with a sponge ball. The chaser attempts to hit "It" with the ball instead of tagging him or her.

FOLK DANCE

Folk dance is considered an art form which depicts the customs and beliefs of a country. Square dances are a form of folk dance of the United States that communicate the culture of early American settlers in the western part of the United States. The following are examples of folk dances that the parachute can be easily adapted to.

You should note that these Folk Dance activities would also be considered "Singing Rhythms" activities. And, as pointed out for the activities listed for "Singing Rhythms", many or some of the following rhythmic singing activities will no doubt be unfamiliar to you and your group. Do not worry about it! Simply have your group say the words out loud. The very fact that they say the words out loud in unison will establish its own rhythmic beat. This is called "chanting". In order to guide the cadence or beat of the "chanting", be sure and have your group say the words with you and follow your lead. (You could even stomp your feet to each word, part-word, every other word, etc.) After several run-throughs with your group, you will find that the chanting experience will create its own beat that will be best for the particular activities suggested.

GREEN COFFEE GROWS

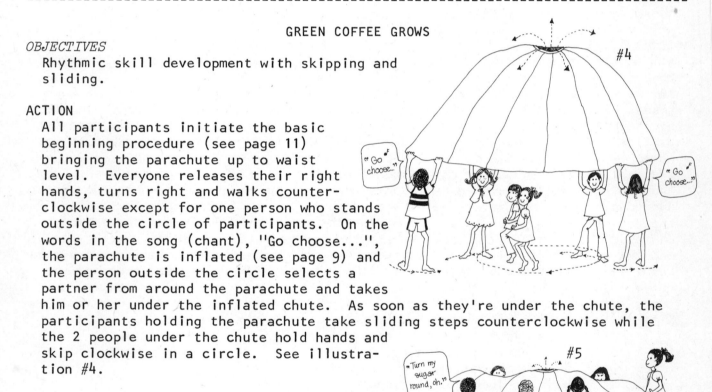

OBJECTIVES
  Rhythmic skill development with skipping and sliding.

ACTION
  All participants initiate the basic beginning procedure (see page 11) bringing the parachute up to waist level. Everyone releases their right hands, turns right and walks counterclockwise except for one person who stands outside the circle of participants. On the words in the song (chant), "Go choose...", the parachute is inflated (see page 9) and the person outside the circle selects a partner from around the parachute and takes him or her under the inflated chute. As soon as they're under the chute, the participants holding the parachute take sliding steps counterclockwise while the 2 people under the chute hold hands and skip clockwise in a circle. See illustration #4.

On the words in the first chorus "Turn my sugar...", the participants holding the parachute change directions and hold the parachute with their right hands. The people under the chute also change directions.

On the words in the 2nd chorus, "Turn my sugar," everyone stops, parachute is deflated while the person who was not holding the parachute originally, now joins the participants holding the chute. The remaining person stands outside of the parachute circle and begins the next dance. See illustration #5.

Sing or chant: Green coffee grows on white oak trees,
                        The rivers flow with brandy, Oh,
                        Go choose you anyone you please
                        And swing like m'lassess candy, Oh.

1st Chorus: Somebody's rocking my sugar lump (say 3 times)
                  Turn my sugar round, Oh.

2nd Chorus: Jus' keep rocking my sugar lump (say 3 times)
                  Turn my sugar round, Oh.

TEACHING HINTS

As a variation, have 2 or more people select a partner and perform the skipping
or other perceptual-motor skills under the parachute.

CIRACASSIAN CIRCLE

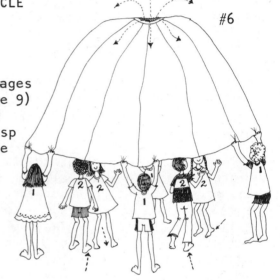

#6

OBJECTIVES
Coordinate skipping skills with rhythms.

ACTION
Have all participants count-off by 2's (see pages
8 to 9). Everyone makes an umbrella (see page 9)
and all the "one's" release the parachute and
take 8 short steps forward and 8 back and grasp
the parachute again. Another umbrella is made
and all the 2's do the same thing. (See illustration #6.) Now make ripples and waves
(see page 10) while skipping 16 steps clockwise and 16 steps counterclockwise in a circle. (Remember to turn and release appropriate hands depending on the circular direction taken.)

TEACHING HINTS
Establish a rhythmic beat for the dance by clapping your hands, stomping feet,
etc. As a variation, you can change walking forwards and backwards and the skipping skills to other perceptual-motor skills such as galloping or a step-step-
step-hop pattern. Also, when the participants walk forward under the parachute,
have them perform another activity such as clapping or have them bow and curt-
sy once they reach the center.

IRISH WASHERWOMAN*

#7

OBJECTIVES
Slide, right and left and hand-stars and
weaving skill developments.

ACTION
All participants initiate the basic beginning procedure (see page 11) bringing
the parachute up to waist level. They

* from Seeker & Jones, 1973

63

all count-off by 2's (see pages 8 to 9). Everyone releases their left hands, turns left and moves clockwise 16 steps (see illustration #7 at the bottom of page 63), then they turn to the right, release their right hands and move 16 steps counterclockwise. Then the parachute is inflated (see page 9) and all the participants who represent one's exchange places with each other by crossing to the opposite side. The parachute is inflated again and all the participants who represent 2's exchange places with each other by crossing to the opposite side. (See illustration #8.) Repeat the 16 clockwise and counterclockwise steps and then make an umbrella (see page 9). All the one's now make a "right-hand-star" by going underneath the parachute's center, touching each other's right hands with their right arms held straight up overhead while walking together clockwise in a circle one complete revolution, then returning to their spots around the chute. Another umbrella is formed and all the 2's form a "left-hand-star" by going underneath the parachute's center, touching each other's left hands with their left arms held straight up overhead while walking together counterclockwise in a circle one complete revolution (see illustration #9), then returning to their spots around the chute.

The 16 clockwise and counterclockwise steps are repeated and another umbrella is formed. This time, moving in a clockwise direction, all the one's weave in and out (around in front of the 1st number 2, behind the 2nd number 2, in front of the 3rd number 2, etc.) until the 4th number 2 is reached whereupon all number one's grasp the parachute again. All form another umbrella and the 2's do what the one's did, but move in a counterclockwise direction. (See illustration #10.)

Repeat the 16 clockwise and counterclockwise steps, form an umbrella, and the one's weave in and out counterclockwise back to their original spots. Form another umbrella and the 2's weave in and out counterclockwise back to their original spots. Finally repeat the 16 clockwise and counterclockwise steps (without weaving in and out) and form a mountain (see pages 10 to 11).

TEACHING HINTS
You can also clap, stamp, tap wood sticks, or play square dance music (since this is perfect as a square dance routine) in the background to establish a rhythmic pattern to do the activities by. If you know them, use other square dance steps under the umbrella such as "do-si-do", etc.

64

CARROUSEL

11

OBJECTIVES

Rhythmic skill development while performing the slide step.

ACTION

Pair everyone around the parachute with one partner holding the parachute at shoulder level after initiating the basic beginning procedure (see page 11). The other person places both hands on their partner's shoulders. Together the partners perform 16 slide steps clockwise followed by 16 slide steps counterclockwise. After the completion of the 32 slide steps, the partners change positions. The inside partner also makes ripples and waves (see page 10) to the song or chant which gradually increases in speed. See illustration #11.

Sing or chant (slowly to begin with):
>   Little children, sweet and gay, Carrousel is running,
>   It will run till evening.
>   Little ones a nickel, big ones a dime.
>   Hurry up, get on board, or you'll surely be too late.

Chorus: Ha, ha, ha, happy are we,
>   Anderson and Peterson and Lundstrom and me!
>   Ha, ha, ha, happy are we,
>   Anderson and Peterson and Lundstrom and me!

TEACHING HINTS

Teach the basic steps first, without singing or chanting. This dance could also be modified by allowing the participants to form a different perceptual-motor skill each 32 steps.

FOUR IN A BOAT

OBJECTIVES

Walking, and basic square dance skill development.

ACTION

All participants, except 4 outside of the parachute circle, initiate the basic beginning procedure (see page 11) bringing the chute up to waist level and hold the parachute with their left hands, turn right and walk counterclockwise. The 4 participants on the outside of the circle walk clockwise. (See illustration #12.) On the words in Verse 1, "Get you a pretty...", each of the 4 participants on the outside select a partner from the parachute's edge as the chute is being inflated (see page 9) and go under the inflated parachute. The 8 participants under the parachute promenade clockwise, swing each other (whatever you want to call a "swing"), then the original 4 participants join the participants around the chute's edge and the other 4 run outside the parachute circle and begin the next dance. While the 8 participants are under the parachute, the participants holding the chute walk counterclockwise. (See illustration #13.)

#13

Verse 1, sing or chant:
4 in a
boat
and the
tide
rolls
high,
4 in
a boat
and the tide
rolls high,
4 in a boat and the tide rolls high,
Get you a pretty one, bye and bye.

Verse 2, sing or chant:
Get me a pretty one, stay all day,
Get me a pretty one, stay all day,
Get me a pretty one, stay all day,
We don't care what the old folks say.

Verse 3, sing or chant:
8 in the boat and it won't go 'round,
8 in the boat and it won't go 'round,
8 in the boat and it won't go 'round,
Swing that pretty one you've just found.

TEACHING HINTS
Try different perceptual-motor skills for participants holding the parachute and a variety of dance steps with the 8 participants under the chute.

KINDERPOLKA

#14

OBJECTIVES
Coordinate sliding, walking, and stamping steps with rhythms.

ACTION
Everyone inflates (see page 9) the parachute and takes 2 steps in, stamps their feet twice and returns to their original spots. Inflate the parachute again and repeat the action. Slide 2 steps clockwise and 2 steps counterclockwise, and then repeat the action. Inflate parachute again and shake it while hopping on the left foot and concurrently put the right foot forward with the big toe up and the heel on the floor. (See illustration #14.) Now perform the same action with the left foot forward. Finally inflate the parachute, stamp feet 3 times, 2 steps in and then back to the original spot.

66

TEACHING HINTS

You can teach the basic skill without music and parachute first. You may incorporate additional polka steps into the dance.

ACADEMIC ACTIVITIES

Basic academic skills may also be
taught through the use of a parachute. This integration of classroom and playground activities will
enable the educator to reinforce academic
concepts with the additional practice and
added motivation that parachute activities
bring. In this manner, concepts learned
in the classroom can be emphasized through
parachute activity. For example, while
learning the effect of gravity and plane-
tary orbits, the "Planetary Jump" and "Gravitational Pull" activities can be u-
tilized to enhance these academic concepts.

Equipment that can be used for parachute activities are 3" x 3" x 1/4" thick pieces
of plywood with colors, geometric shapes, and letters on them, as well as pictures
(public sights, articles of clothing, fruits and vegetables, etc.). In this section, "Academic Activities" will focus on developing skills in reading, science,
mathematics, health and life needs, and form and color recognition.

The general procedure for utilizing academic games with the parachute is as follows: place colored pieces of plywood, for example, under the center of the parachute's aperture. The group raises the parachute making an umbrella (see page 9).
From the time the chute is inflated into an umbrella until it deflates a variety
of academic activities can be performed. These activities are similar to those
described by Cratty (1971) and Wedemeyer and Cejka (1971) with the exception of
the inclusion of the time factor (activities must be completed by an individual
before the parachute descends on him or her). The group leader presents the problem or challenge verbally, or on a card to an individual as the umbrella is formed.
This individual then completes the activity under the parachute before the parachute descends. The following are examples of activities that can be performed
to enhance academic concepts.

PICK-UP

OBJECTIVES
  Color recognition development.

ACTION
  First assign a different color to each participant and place several bean bags in the
  center of the floor under the parachute's
  aperture. When the parachute is inflated
  into an umbrella (see page 9), call a
  color and allow participants of that color to retrieve at least one bean bag
  before the chute touches them or the
  floor. See illustration #1.

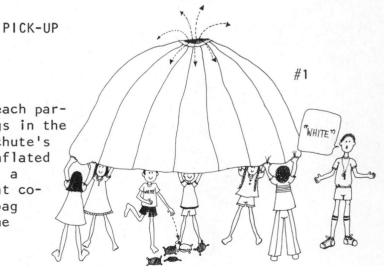

TEACHING HINTS
Present a visual stimulus to participants by having them retrieve objects of a designated color or provide other colored objects in the shape of cats, dogs, etc., to retrieve.

HAVE YOU SEEN MY SHEEP?

OBJECTIVES
Color recognition development.

ACTION
Choose someone to be the "shepherd". Have the remaining participants stand facing the parachute spaced evenly around it. Participants then reach down and grasp the chute's edge with both hands using an overhand grip and bring the chute up to waist level. The "shepherd" walks around the parachute circle and asks: "Has anyone seen my sheep?". The "shepherd" then touches someone in the circle who immediately asks: "How is the sheep dressed?" The "shepherd" responds with a description of one of the participants in the circle such as, "He wears a red shirt and gray pants." The touched participant attempts to identify the sheep as more details are added by the "shepherd". If the touched participant guesses correctly who the described person is, the "shepherd" responds with "Yes," and the touched participant immediately chases the described participant around the circle. If the described participant is tagged before he or she can return to his or her original place, the chaser (touched person) becomes the "shepherd" or else the runner becomes the "shepherd".

TEACHING HINTS
You can vary the skill by having running, hopping, or skipping utilized by the various participants.

OBJECTIVES
Arithmetic development.

ACTION
Everyone initiates the basic beginning procedure (see page 11) bringing the parachute up to waist or chest level. Decide upon a number to be used for the game. For example, if 3 is the number selected, then 3 or any multiple of 3 will have the word "buzz" substituted for it. All participants while jumping, hopping, walking, running, etc., begin in unison to make ripples and waves (see page 10) or merely keep the parachute taunt. Then, starting with the number one, all participants count in sequence around the circle, for example, one, 2, 3, 4, etc., making sure to substitute the word, "buzz", at the mention of 3 or its' multiple. (See illustration #2.) If anyone says the number 3 (or its' multiple) when a "buzz" should be said or uses "buzz" in the wrong place, begin the count again. The number may be changed periodically.

TEACHING HINTS

Vary by allowing participants to move around the circle by running, hopping, etc., while reciting the numbers; use addition, subtraction, etc. Also as participants move around in a circle, give commands to run, then hop, etc., and inflate (see page 9) the parachute and make an umbrella (see page 9) with it, etc.

LETTER GAMES

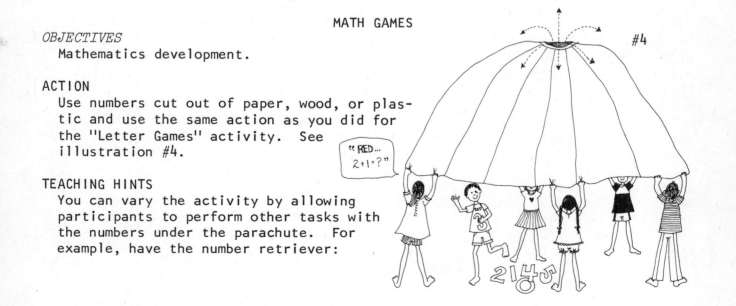

OBJECTIVES
Reading development.

ACTION

First choose a group leader. Have participants inflate (see page 9) the parachute above several letters (cut out of paper, wood or plastic) placed on the floor below the chute's aperture. The group leader calls out a letter and the name or number (if participants have been assigned a number) of one of the participants who then runs to the letters and selects the appropriate letter and returns to his or her place around the chute before it descends and touches the "letter retriever". See illustration #3.

TEACHING HINTS

Vary the activity by allowing participants to perform other tasks with the letters under the parachute. For example, have the letter retriever:
1) Locate and show the other participants the first letter in a name.
2) Match a letter to a sound presented.
3) Spell a word that defines a definition.
4) Spell a word that sounds the same, but is spelled differently from a word spelled on a card.
5) Spell a word that is the opposite of hot.
6) Respond to a spoken word by spelling it as in a "spelling bee".

MATH GAMES

OBJECTIVES
Mathematics development.

ACTION

Use numbers cut out of paper, wood, or plastic and use the same action as you did for the "Letter Games" activity. See illustration #4.

TEACHING HINTS

You can vary the activity by allowing participants to perform other tasks with the numbers under the parachute. For example, have the number retriever:

1) Put the numbers one to 10 in correct order.
2) Show the other participants as many numbers as possible that can be divided by 3.
3) Show the other participants as many numbers as possible that are a multiple of 5.
4) Show the other participants just even (odd) numbers only.
5) Show the other participants the answers to math problems presented by the group leader:

$$2 - 1 = \qquad 2 \times 1 =$$
$$3 - 2 = \qquad 2 \times ? = 2$$
$$2 - ? = 0 \qquad 4 \times ? = 4$$

6) Set up and answer problems presented by the group leader that utilize square root, division, etc., to increase the complexity of the activity.

FIGURE BLOCK COLOR GAMES

OBJECTIVES

Color discrimination and recognition development.

ACTION

Have the participants inflate (see page 9) the parachute over a number of different colored blocks or cards. Call one or more participant's names or assigned numbers and have them locate a color you've designated under the chute and return to their places around the parachute before the chute descends and touches them. Be sure and have them show the colors they've chosen to the other participants around the chute in order to get their agreement on choosing the correct colors.

TEACHING HINTS

You may vary the activity by allowing the participants chosen as color retrievers to perform the following tasks under the inflated parachute:
1) Locate and show the other participants a primary color of brown.
2) Locate and show the other participants a series of colors and put them in the correct color sequence called.
3) Race 2 at a time to find a specific color block.
4) Locate the same color that the group leader shows.

GEOMETRIC FIGURE GAMES

OBJECTIVES

Form recognition development.

ACTION

Have everyone inflate (see page 9) the parachute over a variety of different shapes. When the group leader or another participant shows a shape, select one or more participants to leave their places around the parachute and run under the chute to match the shape shown to one or more similar shapes before the parachute descends and touches them. See illustration #5.

#5

TEACHING HINTS

You can vary the activity by allowing the participants called upon to perform the following tasks under the inflated parachute:
1) Touch and identify as many geometric shapes as possible.
2) Attempt to locate and place in correct order a series of shapes.
3) Attempt to retrieve a shape first (2 participants compete).
4) Attempt to locate pictures of different shaped animals, etc.

MATHEMATICAL NUMBER CHANGE

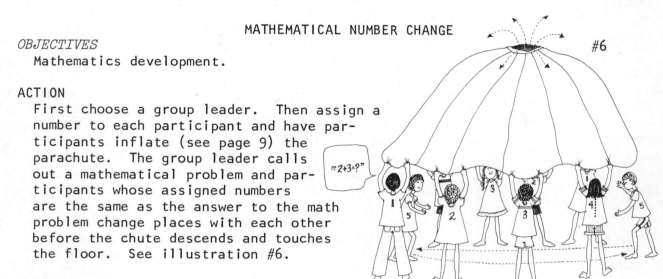

#6

OBJECTIVES
Mathematics development.

ACTION

First choose a group leader. Then assign a number to each participant and have participants inflate (see page 9) the parachute. The group leader calls out a mathematical problem and participants whose assigned numbers are the same as the answer to the math problem change places with each other before the chute descends and touches the floor. See illustration #6.

TEACHING HINTS

You can vary the activity by utilizing a variety of mathematical concepts of addition, subtraction, multiplication, and division. Increase complexity by combining 2 or more mathematical functions to get an answer, for example, $6 + 9 - 5 = 10$, etc.

PICTURE ACTIVITIES

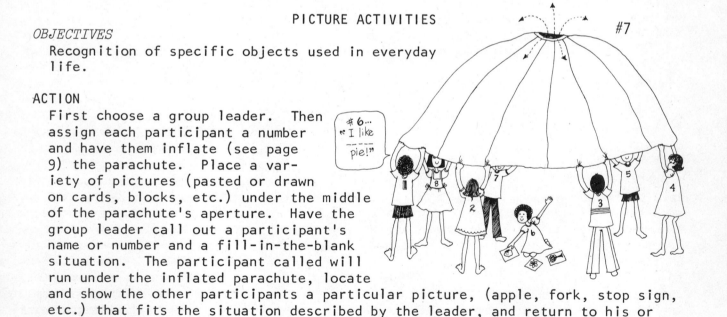

#7

OBJECTIVES
Recognition of specific objects used in everyday life.

ACTION

First choose a group leader. Then assign each participant a number and have them inflate (see page 9) the parachute. Place a variety of pictures (pasted or drawn on cards, blocks, etc.) under the middle of the parachute's aperture. Have the group leader call out a participant's name or number and a fill-in-the-blank situation. The participant called will run under the inflated parachute, locate and show the other participants a particular picture, (apple, fork, stop sign, etc.) that fits the situation described by the leader, and return to his or her place around the parachute before the chute descends and touches him or her. See illustration #7.

TEACHING HINTS
You can vary the activity by providing a variety of tasks for the picture retriever such as:
1) Locate and show other participants 2 pictures that are alike (bicycle and
   car) or different (salt and pepper shakers).
2) Locate and show other participants the picture that goes with the term
   "toothpaste" (illustration of the toothpaste).
3) Locate and show other participants a picture with the same functions as
   a knife (illustration of a saw).

MEMORY QUIZ

OBJECTIVES
Direction memory development.

ACTION
Have participants form an umbrella (see page 9). On the signal, "Go", have
one or more participants exhibit a 5 step routine (2 steps forward and 3 steps
backward) which has bee previously demonstrated by you or a participant.

TEACHING HINTS
You should vary the routine but utilize different: directions, numbers of steps
and sequences. Also initiate the routine on the 2nd, 3rd time, etc., the parachute is inflated.

STEPPING STONES

OBJECTIVES
Number recognition devel'opment.

#8

ACTION
Choose a group leader and create an umbrella (see page 9) over 10 one foot square
stones (made from flat pieces of
rubber mats, carpet remnants, plywood, etc.) that are numbered one
through 10. The group leader calls
on one or more participants to go
under the chute and walk on specific
stones that correspond to a number sequence the leader gives. This must be
done before the parachute descends and
touches the people underneath. See illustration #8.

TEACHING HINTS
You may vary the activity by having the participants jump or hop over the correct stepping stones. (Safety precaution: Make sure the stones do not slip or
slide when participants walk on them.)

DECADE JUMP

OBJECTIVES
Mathematical concept development.

ACTION

Choose a group leader and create an umbrella (see page 9) over a number grid (5 ft long by 5 inches wide) that is marked off in intervals of 10's (10, 20, 30, 40, 50). One or more participants are then selected to jump a series of numbers based on the directions of the group leader before the parachute descends and touches the jumpers. See illustration #9.

TEACHING HINTS

Vary this activity by having 2 participants race each other to see who completes the series first. Hopping could also be substituted for jumping or intervals of 3's or 5's, etc., could be utilized instead of 10's.

PLANETARY JUMP

OBJECTIVES

Science development.

ACTION

Everyone inflates (see page 9) the parachute with you or a selected group leader sitting on the floor underneath the chute's aperture. Bean bags (representing the planets of the solar system) are tied at various points along the length of a rope and whirled around the sun (group leader) in an orbit (circle). The group leader then has one or more participants (meteors) go under the inflated chute and jump over (not colliding with) as many different planets as possible before the parachute comes down. Everyone should try to keep the chute high enough so it does not descend on the leader. See illustration #10.

TEACHING HINTS

Vary the path of the planets by starting low and then increasing the height of their orbits. In addition, participants can step, duck or avoid the planets by any means. (For safety: Bean bags should be soft and light weight or better yet use foam blocks in their places.) You can also ask various action questions which a participant attempts to answer, such as:
  1) Can you collide with (or jump over) the largest (smallest) planet in the solar system?
  2) Jump each of the planets and call out their names.
  3) Which planet has the most moons? Jump it.
  4) Which planet has rings around it? Collide with it or jump it.
  5) Jump the 2 planets nearest to the earth and call out their names.
  6) Jump the planet with the same name as a famous dog 2 times.
  7) Jump or hop over the planet where Superman and ET live.

GRAVITATIONAL PULL

OBJECTIVES

Science development.

#11

ACTION

Have participants initiate the basic beginning procedure (see page 11) bringing the parachute up to waist level. Everyone should stretch the parachute tightly. A circle is drawn inside the circle of participants that is approximately 12 inches in front of each participant's foot. On the signal, "Go", participants simulate the gravitational pull of the moon and the sun and try to pull the other players into the drawn circle. This is similar to "tug-o-war". See illustration #11.

TEACHING HINTS

You can vary by allowing participants to sit on the floor or form teams while performing the activity.

LOOK AND LISTEN

OBJECTIVES

Reading development.

#12

ACTION

First choose a group leader. Have everyone initiate the basic beginning procedure (see page 11) bringing the parachute up to waist level. The group leader presents a letter of the alphabet and calls a word that may or may not begin with that letter sound. (See illustration #12.) If the word does begin with that sound, participants inflate (see page 9) the chute. (See illustration #13.) If the word called does not begin with that particular sound, the participants do nothing.

TEACHING HINTS

You can vary the activity by allowing the participants to run in a circle around the chute, if the word begins with the correct sound. Or, release the parachute and let it fall to the ground, if the word does not begin with the designated sound.

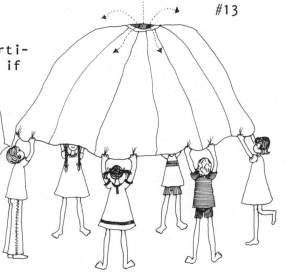

#13

75

OBJECTIVES
General academic development.

ACTION
First choose a group leader. Then have the group leader ask questions related to the functions of the parachute such as what is the purpose of the hole in the parachute. Then allow the participants to inflate and deflate (see page 9) the parachute to demonstrate the answer.

TEACHING HINTS
You can vary the activity by asking a variety of academic questions such as:
1) How do we fill the parachute with air?
2) How hard (soft) can you shake the parachute?
3) How high (low) can you shake the parachute?
4) How can you make the parachute reach sea level? The top of the mountain?
5) How can you shake the parachute like snow (or a leaf) falling?
6) How can you make the parachute like the ocean?
7) How can you make the parachute like the ocean during a storm?

RESOURCES

In the following section are numerous resources. These resources are grouped into 3 categories: 1) Selected Readings, 2) Records, and 3) Equipment And Supplies.

SELECTED READINGS

Evans, D. OH CHUTE: PARACHUTE ACTIVITIES FOR FUN & FITNESS. Sioux Falls, South Dakota: Raven Industries, Inc., 1971

An illustrated instructor's manual on numerous parachute activities which was designed for use by educators and recreators.

Fluegelman, A. MORE NEW GAMES! Garden City, New York: Dolphin Books, 1981.

Additional creative parachute games have been devised to supplement the original text.

Fluegelman, A. (Ed.) THE NEW GAMES BOOK. Garden City, New York: Dolphin Books, 1976.

Innovative parachute games are explained that are appropriate for large groups no matter what age.

Hall, J.T.; Sweeney, N.H.; and Esser, J. UNTIL THE WHISTLE BLOWS. Santa Monica, California: Goodyear Publishing Company, Inc., 1976.

Several manipulative and rhythmic parachute activities are suggested.

Hansen, J. Conditioning and Aerobics for Older Americans. Journal of Physical Education and Recreation. 51, 1980, 20-21.

Several teaching techniques and exercises to improve the physical condition of older citizens are provided. Parachute games are among the activities discussed.

Hayes, A. Using Parachutes to Develop Fitness and Movement Skills. Physical Education Newsletter. 15(6), November 1970.

Henrie, B.C. PARACHUTE PLAY (Rev. Ed.). Berwick, Pennsylvania: Keystone Publishing Company, 1964.

Several basic parachute activities are clearly explained with accompanying photographs.

Jacobson, S. PARACHUTE. Tacoma, Washington: Tacoma Public Schools, no date.

Numerous parachute activities are explained. These activities are categorized in the following areas: lead-up activities, game activities, exercise activities, adapted games activities, and rhythm activities.

Johnson, L.J. Parachute Play For Exercise. Journal of Health, Physical Education and Recreation; 38, 1967, 22-27.

General information on the appropriate use of a parachute is presented. The majority of the article is devoted to isometric exercises and stunts that can be performed with the parachute.

Kirchner, G. PHYSICAL EDUCATION FOR ELEMENTARY SCHOOL CHILDREN. (4th Ed.) Dubuque, Iowa: William C. Brown, 1978.

Several parachute exercises and games explained and illustrated.

Klappholz, L. Try Parachute Activities to Teach Movement Skills and Develop Physical Fitness. The Physical Activities Report. (Issue 406), January 1976, 6-8.

Includes lead-up activities, individual and group games, isometric exercises, stunts and tumbling, rhythms, and safety procedures for elementary, aged, handicapped, and nonhandicapped students.

Langsner, F.R. PARACHUTES. Homer, New York: Things From Bell, no date.

In this booklet numerous physical fitness and perceptual-motor skills as well as rhythm activities are discussed.

Marston, R. FOLK & DISCO PARACHUTE DANCES FOR ELEMENTARY STUDENTS. Sioux Falls, South Dakota: Raven Industries, Inc. 1980.

Numerous disco and folk dances are presented which have been modified for use with a parachute. A dance assessment is included.

Popen, C. and Miller, F. S. Go Parachuting. Journal of Health, Physical Education, and Recreation. 38, 1967, 24-25.

A developmentally sequenced series of parachute activities are presented. These activities involve gymnastic stunts, physical activities, and games.

Using A Parachute to Teach Movement Skills and Develop Overall Physical Fitness. <u>Physical Education Newsletter</u>. Issue 133, January, 1982.

Several parachute lead-up activities, games, isometric exercises, and stunts are explained. One section of the article is devoted to safety procedures.

RECORDS

CHUTE THE WORKS
Develops gross motor skills, coordination, rhythm awareness and manipulative activities. Designed for participants with parachute activity experience. Exercises are coordinated with dynamic music that stimulate "chutists" and gets them "flying high". Side 1 = narration and music; Side 2 = music only.

PARACHUTE ACTIVITIES WITH FOLK DANCE MUSIC
Develops coordination and rhythmic skills through the use of parachute play activities and international folk dance steps. By using the motivational aspects of the parachute, folk dance steps become more exciting. Parachute activities include floating clouds, crossing under the umbrella, inside the mountain, and more. A 2 record album. Sides 1 and 3 = narration and music; sides 2 and 4 = music only.

PARACHUTE ROUNDUP
Develops rhythm and coordination patterns. The music on the record is classified as country rock.

PLAYTIME PARACHUTE FUN
Designed for the 6 foot parachute which can be used in classrooms or limited spaces. An instructor's manual is included.

POP ROCK PARACHUTE
Develops areas of strength, endurance, and flexibility. It allows for the exercise of creative thought through the use of a parachute. Provided in the accompanying manual are descriptions and illustrations of 6 different routines: Circle Tug-O-War, Row The Boat, Bubble Squash, Bombs Away, Bubble House, and Disappear. Motivating, original contemporary music accompanies the activities. Side 1 = narration and music; side 2 = music only.

RHYTHMIC PARACHUTE PLAY
This most popular 2 record album develops gross motor skills through rhythmic exercises by utilizing parachute canopies. Hit tunes provide the background for an instructional record aimed at basic parachute activities and group activities, making ripples and waves, an umbrella, a mountain, a mushroom, merry-go-round, and more. Manual includes suggestions for use and supplementary activities. Sides 1 and 2 = narration and music; sides 3 and 4 = music only.

All of the preceeding parachute record albums are sold by:
Kimbo Educational
10-16 North 3rd Ave.
P.O. Box 477
Long Branch, NJ 07740

With the exception of PARACHUTE ROUNDUP and PLAYTIME PARACHUTE FUN, these parachute records are sold by:

Things From Bell, Inc.   Educational Activities, Inc.
P.O. Box 706   and   P.O. Box 392
Cortland, NY 13045   Freeport, NY 11520

PARACHUTE ROUNDUP and PLAYTIME PARACHUTE FUN is sold by:
Flaghouse, Inc.
18 West 18th St.
N.Y., N.Y. 10011

And last, but not least, the publisher sells the most popular of the parachute albums, namely, RHYTHMIC PARACHUTE PLAY:
Front Row Experience
540 Discovery Bay Blvd.
Byron, CA 94514

EQUIPMENT AND SUPPLIES

There are just a few pieces of equipment and supplies needed to play with a parachute. Most importantly is the parachute itself. A professional who uses the parachute frequently should also obtain a parachute bag and repair tape.

PARACHUTES
    While a parachute is basically a tough nylon fabric with an air release hole or aperture in the center, there are numerous variations in size and color. The following is a listing of some parachute vendors and a brief description of their products. Note that none of the chutes listed are government surplus, but instead are specifically manufactured for parachute activities. You should further note that for safety reasons and to increase the life expectancy of your manufactured parachute, it is not recommended that you use the following chutes to lift heavy objects such as a child or an adult as in a "blanket toss" type game. Also, do not attempt to use your chute in a "tug-o-war" game unless you know your parachute can take it. Generally speaking (although you can not be sure) only a modified government surplus parachute that was actually used (or designed to be used) to drop people and supplies from the air are strong enough for "blanket toss" and vigorous "tug-o-war" activities, but again, do not count on it!

Flaghouse, Inc.   and   Olympia Sports   Parachute is made of
18 West 18th St.   745 State Circle   tough nylon fabric in
N.Y., N.Y. 10011   Ann Arbor, MI 48106   red and white alter-
                                                            nating panels with a
reinforced skirt. The 4 sizes available are 6 ft, 12 ft, 19 ft, and 24 ft diameters.

Front Row Experience
540 Discovery Bay Blvd.
Byron, CA 94514

The publisher offers 6 ft, 12 ft, 20 ft, and 24 ft diameter parachutes. Each chute is made of durable rip-stop nylon with a striking multicolored canopy of red, yellow, and blue panels.

Jayfro, Inc.
P.O. Box 400
Waterford, CT 06385

Play canopy made of high strength nylon parachute fabric. The skirt is reinforced for additional strength. Washable canopies come in bright contrasting colors. The parachutes are 6 ft, 12 ft, and 24 ft diameters.

Snitz Mfg.
2096 South Church St.
East Troy, WI 53120

Parachute constructed of red and white all nylon to withstand heavy school use. The chutes are available in diameters of 6 ft, 12 ft, and 24 ft.

Things From Bell, Inc.
P.O. Box 706
Cortland, NY 13045

4 sizes are available in diameters of 6 ft, 12 ft, 20 ft, and 24 ft. In each size there are 3 qualities, deluxe (rip stop nylon), standard (320 Denier net nylon) and economy (tricot nylon).

U.S. Games, Inc.
P.O. Box EG874   and
Melbourne, FL 32935

Raven Industries, Inc.
P.O. Box 1007
Sioux Falls, SD 57117

Parachute is manufactured of multi-colored rugged nylon rip stop fabric

with reinforced sewing. The canopy comes in 8 sizes: 6 ft, 12 ft, 19 ft, 22 ft, 26 ft, 28 ft, and 32 ft diameters.

PARACHUTE BAG
The parachute bag protects the parachute in storage and carrying. The bag is made of sturdy white canvas and is 16 inches by 20 inches. The following companies are vendors of parachute bags:

Flaghouse, Inc.
18 West 18th St.   and
NY, NY 10011

Snitz Mfg.
2096 South Church St.
East Troy, WI 53120

PARACHUTE REPAIR TAPE
Repair tape can increase the longevity of a parachute. It is a fast, easy way to make patches. Simply cut a piece of tape from the roll, remove paper from adhesive backing, and press over tear. The tape is in a 2 inch by 25 ft roll and can be ordered in red, blue, or white. The following companies sell parachute repair tape:

Raven Industries, Inc.
P.O. Box 1007   and
Sioux Falls, SD 57117

Snitz Mfg.
2096 South Church St.
East Troy, WI 53120

REFERENCES

Cratty, B.J. ACTIVE LEARNING. Englewood Cliffs, NJ: Prentice-Hall, Inc., 1971.

Evans, D. PARACHUTE ACTIVITIES FOR FUN AND FITNESS. Sioux Falls, SD: Raven Industries, Inc., 1971.

French, R. and Jansma, P. SPECIAL PHYSICAL EDUCATION. Columbus, OH: Charles C. Merrill Publishers, 1982.

Gallahue, D.L. and Meadors, W.S. LET'S MOVE. Dubuque, IA: Kendall/Hunt Publishing Co., 1974.

Hansen, S. Conditioning and Aerobics for Older Americans. Journal of Health, Physical Education and Recreation, 52, 1980, 20-21.

Jacobsen, S. PARACHUTE IDEAS. Tacoma, WA: Tacoma Public Schools, 1975.

Johnson, B.L. and Nelson, J.K. PRACTICAL MEASUREMENTS FOR EVALUATION IN PHYSICAL EDUCATION (3rd Ed.). Minneapolis, MN: Burgess Publishing Company, 1979.

Popen, E. and Miller, L.S. Go Parachuting. Journal of Health, Physical Education and Recreation, 38, 1967, 24-25.

Schurr, E. MOVEMENT EXPERIENCES FOR CHILDREN (2nd Ed.). Englewood Cliffs, NJ: Prentice-Hall, Inc., 1980.

Seeker, J. and Jones, G. PARACHUTE ACTIVITIES WITH FOLK DANCE MUSIC. Deal, NJ: Kimbo Educational, 1973.

Wedemeyer,A. and Cejka, J. LEARNING GAMES FOR EXCEPTIONAL CHILDREN. Denver, CO: Love Publishing Co., 1971.

! PARACHUTE MOVEMENT WORKSHOPS !

For Workshops in PARACHUTE MOVEMENT ACTIVITIES and related consultation, contact the authors directly at the following addresses:

Ron French, Ed.D.
Department of P.E.
College of HPER
Texas Woman's University
P.O. Box 2317
Denton, TX 76204

Michael Horvat, Ed.D.
Division of HPERD
University of Georgia
Athens, GA 30602